A VERY NICE GLASS of WINE

A Guided Journal

HELEN McGINN

CHRONICLE BOOKS

SAN FRANCISCO

First published in the United States of America
in 2015 by Chronicle Books LLC.
Originally published in the United Kingdom
in 2013 by Macmillan.

Library of Congress Cataloging-in-Publication Data

McGinn, Helen.
  A very nice glass of wine : a guided journal / Helen McGinn.
     pages cm
  ISBN 978-1-4521-2797-2 (alk. paper)
1. Wine and wine making. I. Title.

TP548.M4674 2014
641.2'2--dc23

2014027288

ISBN 978-1-4521-2797-2

Manufactured in China

Designed by Cat Grishaver

Visit Helen McGinn at knackeredmotherswineclub.com
and @knackeredmutha.

10 9 8 7 6 5 4 3 2 1

Chronicle Books LLC
680 Second Street
San Francisco, California 94107
www.chroniclebooks.com

4

INTRODUCTION

8

Getting Started

16

How Wine is Made

24

How to Taste Wine

34

About White Wine

48

About Red Wine

56

Matching Food and Wine

62

How to Buy Wine

68

The Last Drop

Introduction

*T*his guided journal will help you explore, discover, and, ultimately, choose wine with confidence. It's about ensuring that when you do decide to settle down with a glass of wine after a busy day, it's going to be worth it. On the shelf in my study at home is a row of long-ago-emptied wine bottles, each one marked with a date and occasion in silver pen, including a bottle of 1988 vintage Champagne that marks the year the Husband and I got together as teenagers. It was a wedding present and we imbibed it years later, to celebrate the birth of Eldest Boy. I haven't been lucky enough to have it since, but I'll never forget how I felt when I drank it. The thing is, I love wine. Really love it. And I don't just mean what's in the glass. Obviously that's a really big part, and I love that there's always more to discover, but for me wine is about so much more than that. It's about bringing us together around a table. Wine makes us sit down (I especially like that part) and converse. Wine connects us with places, with stories, and, best of all, with each other. Almost twenty years ago I decided I'd like to make my working way in the world with glass in hand, literally, because I liked what was in the glass. Now, a few years on, I can see that it wasn't just about that; it was as much about the people—those who make wine and those who drink it. One of my favorite nights in my not-particularly-social calendar these days is my book-club evening. Sure, we talk about the book, but really it's about a group of friends getting together around a table, sharing funny, sad, mad, and sometimes very bad stories, mixed in with opinions, food, and—of course—a really nice glass of wine.

I've spent my entire working life in the wine industry, feeling for much of it that, like Charlie Bucket, I'd won the Golden Ticket. For years I was a supermarket wine buyer. When the first of my three children came along, I gave up the travel for the travel cot, and now work part time in wine. Friends have always asked me for wine recommendations, whether it's for everyday drinking, slightly posh dinners, parties, weddings, christenings/naming days, anniversaries, or big birthdays ending in a zero. And they've always told me how the great wall of wine they face each week in the market can feel utterly overwhelming. Consequently, for years I sent a regular email to friends who'd asked for recommendations, especially on good wine deals, and the title of that email was "The Knackered Mother's Wine Club." And that was where it all started; the blog was born one night when the Husband was away and I'd had enough of working late with the laptop on the sofa. I thought that sharing my own weekly wine purchases—two wines a week, whatever I happened to be drinking—might help inspire others to try something different as well as unearth some hidden gems and properly good deals along the way.

I blogged every week—usually with a glass within reach—whatever my mood: happy, not so happy, or just plain knackered. For the first few months the blog was read religiously; by my sister, mother, and the Husband. Then I started to get comments from people who were (a) not related to me and (b) seemingly normal, interested in wine, and wanting to know more about it. And so the weekly posts continued, with added video blogs and tasting tips, among other stuff. I received emails from women telling me they'd never realized Chablis was made from Chardonnay grapes (fact) or that "legs" on a glass was a sign of alcohol content rather than quality. In short, my blog had hit on something. These were busy, knowledge-thirsty women, reading my blog and enjoying learning more about wine. It was a revelation. My audience started to grow and suddenly there I was, doing what I love, namely sharing my thoughts on good wine and helping others grow in confidence when choosing, buying, and talking about wine, while encouraging them to try new things.

How I drink now is very different from how I drank before I had children, not least because looking after children with a hangover is rarely worth the pain. More than that, as I get older I'm realizing, actually, I don't want to drink as much as I used to. The shallow part of me worries about the extra calories I'm taking on; the less shallow part of me knows that it isn't good for my general health. The recommended weekly allowance is about seven glasses of wine a week, depending on the strength of the wine and the size of the glass. Pre-children, that was my weekend right there (sound familiar?). Nowadays, I go wine-free at least two nights a week. Overall, I drink less but I drink better. By that, I mean that instead of drinking the same wine week in, week out, I shop around and try different things whenever possible. With so much choice on the shelves and online, you could try a different wine every week and still taste only the tip of the wine-iceberg. I hope that the information in this journal will help you step outside your wine comfort zone and give you the knowledge you need to get more from your glass of wine, to lead you by the hand—or perhaps the nose—through what to drink with Sunday roasts, for book-club tastings, TV dinners, and more. You will feel inspired not to drink more wine, but to drink *better* wine. I'm going to help you think about tasting wines properly, learn how to make tasting notes, and not feel like a pretentious wine-freak writing down what you do and don't like.

Wine is an excellent thing. After a typical hectic day I don't have the mental capacity for much beyond a glass of wine and easy conversation. This guided journal is about helping you understand more about wine so that, seeing as you are probably drinking less than you used to, you make each glass count and drink better.

GETTING Started

I don't have a glass of wine every evening, but more often than not I do. And if I'm going to have a glass of wine, I want it to be one worth drinking; not something that is instantly forgettable. Buying the same afford-able Pinot Grigio week in, week out, might give us the bargain-hit we crave, but it doesn't give us a thrill on the tongue. I'd rather open a better-than-average bottle during the week and make it last longer than have a cheap wine I don't mind drinking.

How much do you need to spend? The wines in my fridge door and in the wine rack change every week. I have become an expert at shopping around, finding good deals, and avoiding bad ones (sadly, some really are too good to be true—more on that later).

It follows that as the cost of the bottle rises, so does the quality of the wine. This is not always the case, but generally it's true. When you think how much you might spend nowadays on a cup of coffee or some emergency chocolate, good wine seems cheap by comparison. Obviously, only you know how much you are willing to spend and if that wine is worth it to you. I generally shop for wine priced between $8 and $25, depending on what the wine is for and what my budget is.

When it comes to selecting our fridge-door whites and in-the-wine-rack reds, these are wines we're likely to drink at home during the week, rather than wines we might bring when eating with friends or family on the weekend (which we'll come to later). This is about how to have wines on hand that are a delight to drink, not just something that is consumed and forgotten. Given that all wine starts the same way, as a grape on the vine, we need to explore what makes wines taste so very different. That way you can start to navi-gate your way around, allowing you to find the good stuff and avoid the bad.

What's in a Wine?

Grapes: Whoever thought so much joy could come from such a small but perfectly formed fruit? Each grape just hangs out on the vine until ripe, ready to be picked and popped into our mouths—unless they are picked to make wine, which is obviously much more fun. Grapes are made up largely of **water**. It's all the other stuff in there that makes the grape great for wine. There are **natural sugars**; there are **flavors** that vary depending on the variety; and there is **natural acidity**. Another ingredient delivered with that little package is **tannin**.

What is Tannin?

Tannin is one of the ingredients—a **polyphenolic compound**, to give its proper definition—that makes up a grape. They are found on the skins, stalks, and seeds of a grape, and how tannins are managed during the winemaking process has a very big influence on the resulting wine. If you are wondering what I mean by "tannin," think of the feeling you get in your mouth when you take a sip of that cup of tea you made, the one where you got distracted by something or someone (probably small), and by the time you got back to your tea the tea bag had been in for a bit too long, leaving it stewed and lukewarm. The relevant thing to remember is the bitter, astringent character of that fated cuppa. I realize I'm not selling tannin well here, but in wine it plays a crucial role as it preserves the wine, enabling it to age well. When making red wine, the skins of the grapes are left in contact with the clear (almost always clear, no matter what the color of the grape is) juice so that color (a.k.a. **anthocyanins**) and tannins can be extracted. Generally, the thicker the skin of the grape, the more color and tannin it will give to the grape juice.

Tannins come in different guises: **"Big" tannins** are often found in wines that are big in every other way, especially fruit and alcohol, such as New World Cabernet Sauvignon and Shiraz, and Malbec from Argentina. **"Firm"** is a word often used to describe a wine where the tannins are very obvious, perhaps even a little harsh, as is sometimes found in very young wines. **"Soft" tannins** are found in wines made from grapes with thinner skins, such as Gamay, Merlot, or Pinot Noir, so the resulting tannins are lighter than their thick-skinned friends.

The best way to understand the difference tannins make to a wine is to try a "big" tannin wine next to a "soft" tannin wine; take a French Pinot Noir and taste it next to an Australian Shiraz. Be sure to taste the Pinot Noir first, then the Shiraz. Note how different the wine feels in weight. Obviously there are loads of other differences to take into account, such as the fruit characters, how much alcohol they have, or whether they have been aged in oak barrels (since these also add tannin to a wine), but the "feel" of the tannins will be incredibly different.

The essential ingredient is, of course, **alcohol**. Alcohol isn't in a grape when picked, but when nature's party trick happens, otherwise known as **fermentation**, yeasts convert the natural sugars in the grape to alcohol.

Oak, or rather the flavor of oak, is another ingredient that might be found in a wine. If a wine is aged in oak barrels, flavors and tannins from the oak will shape the wine over time. Oak is often wine's walking stick, allowing it to age gracefully and keeping it standing much longer than it otherwise would. So there we go. **Water**, **sugar**, **flavors**, **acidity**, **tannin**, **alcohol**, and sometimes **oak** are what's in a wine. We'll explore all of them in more detail as we go, but for now, that's a good place to start.

Where in the World?

Billions of bottles of wine are made around the world every year, and they are often categorized as being either from the **Old World** (meaning, generally speaking, wines from European countries) or from the **New World** (meaning wines from everywhere else, including Australia, New Zealand, Chile, Argentina, and South Africa). Someone once described the difference in terms of style: Old World for more subtle wines, New World for more robust, fruity wines. While this is partly true, as a wine buyer I'd meet French winemakers in Chile, Chilean winemakers in New Zealand, and Australian winemakers in France. Actually, the most obvious difference between the Old World and New World is one you can see rather than taste. It's the way the wines are labeled. Historically, wines from France, Spain, Italy, and other European countries have labeled their wines depending on **place** rather than **grape**, giving top billing on the front labels to the place where the grapes are grown rather than the grape variety. For example, Rioja, Chablis, and Gavi are all places; they are wine-producing regions. If you take a look at a wine from Australia, New Zealand, South Africa, Chile, or Argentina, you'll find the name of the grape variety writ large on the front label. So it helps if you know your grape varieties and your places. However, there are thousands of different grape varieties and wine regions all over the world. I don't plan to tell you about all of them, but I do want to teach you how to navigate the world wine map.

Arguably, we have too much choice, leaving us cowering before a great wall of wine, wishing for a sign to point us in the right direction. Unfortunately, help is not always at hand and we're left to go on label, and previous experience, alone. In which case, it's good to know how to decode a label. Here's what to look for when you pick up a bottle of wine:

DOMAINE McGINN

Meursault

Appellation Meursault Contrôlée

2010

75CL

13.5%

PRODUIT DE FRANCE

A: Producer
B: Region of origin
C: Vintage/year of grape harvest
D: Volume
E: Country of origin
F: Alcohol by volume

A — 2012

B — *Little Mieke*

C — PINOT GRIS

D — *Hazelwood Vineyard*

E — WILLAMETTE VALLEY

F — 750 ML   12% ABV — G

A: Vintage/year of grape harvest
B: Producer
C: Grape variety
D: Where the grapes are from
E: Region/country of origin
F: Volume
G: Alcohol by volume

Off to the Market

Write down the country and grape for each style of wine listed below, and take the list shopping, whether that's at a supermarket, a wine specialist, or an online retailer. Search for some of these wines and see what you find. If you can't find the grape, try a different grape or something from another region in the same country at a similar price.

COLOR: White
STYLE: Crisp
COUNTRY: Italy (Campania region)
GRAPE: Falanghina
WHY CHOOSE IT: Dry, refreshing, undemanding but lovely
PRICE: $12 to $18

COLOR: White
STYLE: Fruity
COUNTRY: Chile (Casablanca region)
GRAPE: Viognier
WHY CHOOSE IT: Bright and sunshiny, with pineapple fruit
PRICE: $12 to $17

COLOR: White
STYLE: Smooth
COUNTRY: New Zealand (Gisborne region)
GRAPE: Chardonnay
WHY CHOOSE IT: Ripe and round, perhaps with a bit of oak
PRICE: $12 to $17

COLOR: Rosé
STYLE: Cheerful
COUNTRY: Spain (Navarra region)
GRAPE: Garnacha
WHY: Juicy, lively, and easy drinking
PRICE: $12 to $17

COLOR: Red
STYLE: Easygoing
COUNTRY: France (Beaujolais region)
GRAPE: Gamay
WHY: Light, bright, and friendly
PRICE: $10 to $17

COLOR: Red
STYLE: Juicy
COUNTRY: Italy (Sicily)
GRAPE: Nero d'Avola
WHY: Ripe, juicy, and crammed with berry fruit
PRICE: $12 to $17

COLOR: Red
STYLE: Bold and beautiful
COUNTRY: Argentina (Mendoza region)
GRAPE: Malbec
WHY: Bit of a show-off but great fun
PRICE: $12 to $17

When shopping, I check out the sales before looking at the rest of the wine aisle. The problem is, the choice of wines on sale gets a bit samey, so I urge you to move on from the bargains if you've tried the wines before. If you're in the supermarket, look at the labels, scan for the country, place, grape variety, and vintage. Read the story on the back label. I know this means slowing down the shopping dash just a bit, but it's time well spent. It's likely it will just be you and at least 500 labels to look at, with a few bits of information scattered around on the shelves. If, however, you are in a specialty wine shop, ask the person behind the counter what they recommend. Ask them if they have tried it themselves—they probably have. The people who work in wine shops are usually abnormally obsessive about wine, so give them an opportunity to help you explore their range and see what happens. The last time I did that in my local wine shop, I left with an Italian red made from a grape I'd never tried (or even heard of) and it was utterly delicious. It is worth asking if you can try it before you buy—you never know. They might be happy to open a bottle if they think others might want to try it.

The idea behind this exercise is to give you a starting point and to get you thinking about wine and being open to trying new things. If you don't like it, that's fine. But you need to try it—perhaps a few times—before saying no. Off you go.

There are thousands of grape varieties grown all over the world. We've started with just a few, but we're in it for the long run.

HOW *Wine* is MADE

*T*his is a bit of a crash course, but here's my guide to how wine is made. Funnily enough, there is more to it than getting some ripe grapes, squashing them, adding yeast, and hoping for the best. I know this technique is still employed by many who fancy themselves as a bit of a winemaker (my brother-in-law included), but I have tasted "Chateau Coach House" and, trust me, it could burn a hole in your throat.

Modern-day winemaking means that winemakers are capable of making the very best from nature's party trick. The main aim when making a wine is to preserve the natural fruit flavors of the grape, and so it follows that really good wine can be made only from really good grapes. White wines are made by picking the grapes, crushing, and pressing them to get the juice out, then fermenting them without the skins. This is because the grape juice is clear; it is the skins that give the resulting wine its color. White wine needs to be made without the skins so the juice stays clear and the resulting wine stays white.

Red wine is made differently. The juice of red grapes is also clear, but letting it ferment with the skins of the grapes gives the juice color. Red grapes will be crushed and sometimes left to macerate (left in contact) with their skins so the juice can take up more of the color and tannin from the skins before fermentation. Some wines are made using natural yeasts, that is, yeasts found on the skins of the grapes. However, this makes the fermentation process a tad unpredictable, so many winemakers now add manufactured yeasts for a little more predictability and to help it along. The juice, skins, and yeasts are left to ferment, usually in large stainless-steel tanks or concrete vats and sometimes, for the very brave (due to the cost and slightly less predictable results), in (usually) oak barrels. Fermentation temperatures need to be carefully controlled, ensuring they don't get too hot (when flavors might be lost) or too cold (when fermentation might stop).

The juice needs to warm up enough to allow fermentation to happen, which is usually at about 55 degrees Fahrenheit or above. The fermentation may take anywhere from a few days to a few weeks depending on what's being made; and if it's a red wine, the skins and juice will be mixed up to ensure the juice takes on the color of the skins. Most wines are then filtered and fined (any unwanted bits taken out) to be ready for bottling, unless the winemaker has decided to stick it in barrels to age it a bit more, in which case off it goes to do its thing (again, more of that later).

What Affects the Flavor of Wine?

Whereas the ingredients list for wine is incredibly short, the list of things that can affect the flavor of a wine is not. These include (1) the grape variety, (2) where it's grown, (3) how it's grown, and (4) who made it. All these things will determine the end flavor. There are thousands of grape varieties, and they can vary from very aromatic to downright dull. They can produce huge bunches of big, juicy grapes or tight little bunches of tiny grapes. And the color of the grapes can vary from the palest yellow to inky black. Where the vine is grown affects how the grape will grow. There are vineyards that lie close to the sea, brushed over daily by sea breezes;

then there are the picture-perfect vineyards that lie on gently sloping hills, like those in the Côte d'Or in Burgundy (where one day I shall retire, drink Pinot Noir, and eat stinky cheese for breakfast if I so wish). More dramatically, there are vineyards that nestle in the foothills of mountain ranges, as in Chile and Argentina. Grapes need about 1,500 hours of sunshine to ripen, black grapes needing a bit more than white. If a vineyard is near the sea or high up in mountain foothills, the cooler air will slow down the ripening process, allowing the grape to develop distinctive varietal characters. If a grape ripens too quickly, the end result may be a wine with lots of alcohol but not enough acidity.

What is Terroir?

This is a French word with no direct translation. The best I can do is "soil," but that doesn't do it, really. "**Terroir**" is a reference to the actual place where a grape is grown, the combination of soil, aspect of the vineyards, and climatic conditions. In fact, everything outside of the winemaker's control is one way to think of it. It can't be easily defined in a word, as it's a combination of factors, so it's not a word you'll find on the label. However, some wines do use the name of a distinctive character such as **silex** (a type of soil found in the Sancerre region) on the label.

Rules Rule, Okay?

Tradition is a big thing in wine. Over time, traditions develop for seemingly no other reason than the fact that this is how it has always been done. Wine traditions have shaped what variety is grown where and how a particular wine from a particular region must be made, down to how many grapes can be taken from the vine to make wine, time spent aging in oak barrels, and what goes on the labels. This is largely an Old World thing, resulting in rules and regulations being put in place to protect these traditions. In France, the Appellation Contrôlée system works to do just that. Spain, Italy, and most other European wine-producing countries have their own rules and regulations, and now the rest of the world is following suit. Rules can be good when it comes to enforcing, or rather protecting, wine quality. If you see the letters "**AC**" (for French wine), "**DO**" (for Spanish) or "**DOC**" (for Italian wine) on the label, it tells you that the wine has been made according to the traditions and rules of a particular region. Finally, there is the way the wine is made, what the winemakers do to it. Depending on where it is made and what is allowed according to local rules, they might put it into oak barrels, or add some sugar to it, or even take some alcohol out of it, and all these things will affect the flavor.

A Word about Sulfites

As it stands, wine doesn't require a list of ingredients on the back label, apart from "contains **sulfites**." What this means is a small amount of sulfur-based chemicals are added to the wine in order to stop it from **oxidizing** (going brown). Sulfites are used in all sorts of food groups as a preserving agent, including dried fruits, processed meats, french fries, and ketchup. All wines contain at least a small amount of sulfites as they're a natural result of the fermentation process. What isn't on the label is the other stuff, apart from grapes, that is used to make wine. That might include yeast, tartaric acid (the same stuff usually found in baking soda), and tannin additions (usually in powder form). If you want to buy a wine whose ingredients are nothing but grapes, then you need to give natural wines a try.

Sulfur in Wines Causes a Hangover

Sulfur is used in winemaking as a tool to keep air away from the unfermented grape juice and resulting wine, so the liquid in question won't oxidize.

Think of the flesh of an apple, freshly bitten into. If you leave it on the table for a while and then come back to take another bite, the flesh will have started to brown. This is because oxygen has come into contact with the flesh and the flesh has oxidized as a result.

Sulfur acts as a barrier to oxygen and means the wine is kept fresh and not exposed to the risk of oxidation. Some people think the levels of sulphur in wine might be the cause of headaches, but the levels found are so very low that's unlikely to be the case. Open a pack of dried apricots and there's more than forty times the sulfur in there than in a glass of wine. The reason for that headache is drinking wine without eating enough food or imbibing enough water at the same time. There has been research to link headaches with levels of naturally occurring histamines in wine, but again this is far from substantiated, and a very clever doctor friend of mine says it's tosh. So, it's probably not the sulfur that's giving you the headache. It's the wine. The secret is to drink lots of water and eat food (but perhaps not apricots).

What Makes a Wine Lower in Alcohol?

If you don't want to go completely booze-free but like the idea of drinking significantly lower-alcohol wines (wines with less than 9 percent alcohol by volume), there are a growing number of wines available, made in different ways. The first is made by picking the grapes early, when sugar levels are lower than they might reach if left to ripen. As sugar is fermented to alcohol (remember that bit?), lower sugar will mean lower alcohol in the resulting wine. However, picking the grapes early means acidity levels will be higher than if the grapes were picked later, which is fine as long as you are in the mood for crisp rather than ripe fruity wine. Another way to achieve naturally lower alcohol levels is to stop the fermentation before it has completely finished naturally. Again, this means lower resulting alcohol, but it also means higher natural sweetness, as there is more sugar left in the wine. So you get lower alcohol but more sweetness. There is a third way, and that is removing the alcohol from the wine. Progress is a wonderful thing, and we now have the technology to do this via various machines, but the quality of these wines varies enormously. Some that I have tasted, at around 8 percent, taste like wine, just not as I know it. Light but not that fresh and definitely lacking in flavor, which isn't what I'm after. But these wines are getting better all the time, so I'll keep trying them. In the meantime, you could add water, or soda, and make a spritzer. If I'm going to have a lovely, light glass of wine, I look for grape varieties that are able to produce wines with alcohol levels below 12 percent, naturally, like Melon de Bourgogne and Riesling.

What are Natural Wines?

Natural wines are those made with as little intervention as possible, either in the vineyard or in the winery. The movement dates back to the 1970s, particularly to the Loire and Beaujolais regions of France, but it's grown to embrace winemakers all over who want to do things as naturally as possible. The wines are usually made from organically or even **biodynamically** grown grapes (sort of superorganic, if you like, a more holistic approach), meaning, ideally, no chemicals or additives. However, some are more "natural" than others, depending on the winemaker. Some may choose to add a bit of sulfur dioxide when they bottle the wine to keep it fresh, and some use cultivated rather than wholly natural yeasts. The point is, the wine is usually made in small quantities and is often fairly unique in taste. Some of the natural white wines I've tried are a bit ciderlike for me, and some of the reds remind me a little too much of that not-so-lovely country smell you get at manure-spreading time, but generally the really good ones are

exactly that: really good wines. The fact that they are natural is even better. The problem is finding them—you'll need to venture beyond the supermarket shelves for these wines—but such is the interest in the natural wine movement that more and more independent wine shops are getting behind them. You're looking at spending at least $15 on a bottle, and whatever you do, don't leave these ones in the wine rack for too long. They need to be consumed young to be at their best.

ABOUT BUBBLY

What makes wine bubbly? There are a number of ways to get those bubbles in a bottle. The traditional—and most expensive—method is by adding a bit more yeast to wine in a bottle, sealing it, and letting it undergo a second fermentation in the bottle. This double fermentation process creates tiny bubbles (CO_2), and if the bottle is sealed, then obviously the bubbles can't escape. Instead, they stay in the wine, adding sparkle.

Champagne is made this way, along with other sparkling wines around the world, including Cava. If made this way, the dead yeast cells, called lees, need to be removed from the bottle before it's sold. This is done by riddling (slowly moving the bottles by hand or machine) so that the lees end up collecting in the top of the bottle. The tops of the bottles are then frozen and the ice cube containing the lees is popped out, the bottles topped up with the desired sugar dose (or **dosage**, as it's known in Champagne), and resealed. Hence the price.

A cheaper way to make sparkling wine is to do the second fermentation in a tank and then bottle the wine under pressure to keep the bubbles. This is known as the **tank method** or **Charmat method**, named after the man who invented it. This is how Prosecco is made, accounting for the softer bubbles (and cheaper production costs).

Then there's the **bicycle-pump method** (the technical term is "carbonation," but I prefer "bicycle pump"), the premise being that you get a tank full of wine and pump bubbles into it. The end result is fairly coarse, big bubbles that dissipate quickly, but bubbles nonetheless. This method is used to make cheap—and sometimes not very cheerful—sparkling wines.

Choosing Bubbly

When it comes to choosing sparkling wines (indeed any wines) for a crowd of people without it costing the earth, you need to do a bit of research. Do an online trawl to see what's on sale at various supermarkets and wine shops, and sign up for e-newsletters while you're there (they're a brilliant way to get advance warning when a good sale comes along, which is essential when buying in bulk). But to save yourself time and money, it helps if you know what are the main types of wine with bubbles.

CAVA
Style: Usually dry or off-dry and fruity
Country: Spain (mostly in the Penedès region)
Grape: A blend of some or all Xarel-lo, Parellada, Macabeo, Chardonnay
Price: $10 to $25
For parties: A bit hit-and-miss, but find a good one, especially vintage, and you're laughing

CHAMPAGNE
Style: Sharper than Cava, more serious
Country: France (Champagne region)
Grape: A blend of some or all Chardonnay, Pinot Meunier, Pinot Noir
Price: At least $30 at full price
For parties: More expensive, but worth it if you can afford it

PROSECCO
Style: Light, easygoing, simple
Country: Italy (Veneto region)
Grape: Glera (usually called Prosecco)
Price: $17 to $20
For parties: Brilliant for parties, especially daytime ones

OTHER SPARKLING WINES
Style: Often use traditional Champagne grapes. Usually dry, crisp, fruity, and good value
Country: Australia, South Africa, New Zealand, Chile, Argentina, England
Grape: Can be anything!
Price: $13 to $40, with price depending on where it's from
For parties: Much more variable, but good ones can be perfect for parties

A note on quantities: It's always better to over-cater than run out. When calculating quantities for parties, you need to allow for a glass per person. Work on six glasses per bottle. With some people driving and some compensating, this usually covers it. At my own wedding, my father was very impressed with his carefully worked-out quantity calculations, as we had only four bottles of Champagne left at the end. What he didn't know was that my brother was last seen at 2 a.m., loading a car up with all the leftover full cases before disappearing off to finish it with friends in a nearby barn. Apparently it was quite an after-party.

HOW to Taste WINE

I do a lot of wine tasting as part of my job. This involves both vertical tastings (wines from the same producer but made in different vintages) and horizontal tastings (wines from different producers in the same region from the same year), although a horizontal tasting after hours usually involves a sofa rather than writing tasting notes.

Even when tasting professionally, I employ the same approach that I do at home, namely: look, smell, taste. It sounds perfectly straightforward, but how many times do you pick up a glass and just take a sip without giving the smell much thought? If you do take a slug without swirling and sniffing the wine, you miss out on about two-thirds of what that wine has to offer. This is because tasting a wine is actually more about smelling it than tasting it.

But before you sniff, open your eyes and look at what's in your glass, which is hopefully something from the list in the first chapter.

Look

The first thing to do is look at the wine. Really look at it, properly, against a white background if possible, so you can see the color as clearly as possible. For white wine, think about the color: Is it pale yellow or straw-colored? The darker it is, the older it might be. For red, it's the other way round, with garnet or brick-colored reds usually being older than the inky-black young guns. Make sure your glass is less than half full, ideally about a third full in fact, and give it a really good swirl to release the aromas. If you happen to have a small, tulip-shaped wineglass, then you've got a perfectly shaped glass for tasting. Otherwise, any normal-size wineglass will do, as long as it's (a) really clean and free of any soapy scents and (b) not more than a third full.

Smell

Next, swirl it around, shove your nose right in the glass, and take a good, long sniff. By doing this, you are giving the hundreds of receptors inside your nose the opportunity to do their thing and send messages to the brain about what it is you're smelling, be it citrus fruits, black fruits, red fruits, spice, oak, or whatever else you might find in there.

As you sniff, your brain is flicking through a Rolodex of listed descriptors, trying to recognize what's in the glass. That's why it's worth spending a bit of time building up your flavor contacts so that you can adequately describe it, even if it's just mentally, to yourself. (It's best not to be drenched in perfume when doing this. The same goes for hair spray.) Here is a simple "nose guide" that points to the main groups found in wine:

FRUITY SMELLS
Citrus
Tropical
Berry
Dried fruits

VEGGIE SMELLS
Herby
Grassy
Green pepper
Minty

BREADY SMELLS
Yeasty

FLORAL SMELLS
Orange blossom
Jasmine

SPICY SMELLS
Pepper
Cloves
Cinnamon
Licorice

WOODY SMELLS
Smoky
Oaky
Vanilla

EARTHY SMELLS
Old socks
Musty
Moldy

WEIRD SMELLS
Eggy
Burnt match
Cardboard

Taste

Finally, take a small amount of wine in your mouth and swill it around, preferably pulling in a little bit of air at the same time. (If you have no idea what I'm talking about, have a look at the video I've done on my blog, knackeredmotherswineclub.com, which is titled, not-so-imaginatively, "How to taste wine." And apologies for the wink to camera; I've no idea why I do this when I'm on camera.) It takes time and dedicated practice not to look ridiculous while doing this, so don't be surprised if your first attempt results in spitting the wine out over the person sitting opposite you. In fact, probably wise not to attempt this for the first time when sitting opposite someone, unless you don't like them much.

Purse your lips, suck in air through a tiny hole, and knock the wine around the mouth. Coat your tongue, gums, and back of the mouth and let the taste buds on your tongue (you've got about 9,000 of them) get their fill. Think about the fruit flavors, the **zip** (a.k.a. **acidity**), the **grip** (a.k.a. **tannins**), the **oomph** (a.k.a. **body**), and the **balance** and **structure**. Of course, you don't have to think about any of those things, just decide whether you like it or not, but taking the time to taste a wine properly like this does make a huge difference in how you'll feel about the wine afterward and also how you'll remember it. You don't have to do this almost ceremonial act every time you take a sip—it makes a fairly unattractive noise and you risk looking a bit weird—but it's definitely worth doing if you want to get properly acquainted with the wine.

WHAT IS THE DIFFERENCE BETWEEN TASTE AND FLAVOR?

Taste is all about characteristics in food, wine, whatever, which we can measure using our palates (our tongue). We can taste four distinct sensations: bitterness, sweetness, saltiness, and acidity. Then there's umami, now widely recognized as the fifth taste, and best described as savoriness or even deliciousness. *Umami* is a Japanese word and describes a flavor found in foods like mushrooms, soy sauce, oily fish, and ripe fruits. Oysters are rich in umami (as is breast milk, apparently).

Flavor involves smell; it's a more complex, personal perception than taste and allows taste and smell to work together to create a unique flavor sensation. This helps explain why some people are more sensitive to certain flavors than others, because the way our sense of smell and taste interact is unique to each one of us. In fact, unless you are an identical twin, you are the only person in the world to smell like you do. I don't mean how you *smell*, I mean how *you* smell.

How Do You Describe Wine?

Wine is often described with specific words and some general face-pulling and arm-waving, even by the experts. The "expert" dictionary includes words like **structure**, **weight**, **balance** and **mouth-feel**, giving us a framework to describe a wine and assess its quality. For example, a wine might be described as having great structure, with balance.

What this means is that the components of the wine—fruit, sugar, alcohol, and tannin—work well together; they are balanced; one single component doesn't shout over another. If the components don't strike a natural balance—the fruit is shouted down by the oaky character, say, or the alcohol leaves a hot sensation in the mouth, the wine just doesn't work as well. Essentially, it's all about balance.

Even though you don't need to know the full dictionary of expert words, it's useful to have an understanding of some of these terms so that you can describe what it is you are tasting beyond just the fruit characteristics. Here's a guide to what some of the most commonly used "winey" words mean. (Warning: They sound quite poncy.)

Balance: A way of describing how the different parts—alcohol, sweetness, acidity, and tannins—sit together in the wine.

Body: This is mostly to do with alcohol and sugar but is a reference to how it feels in the mouth; that is, is it full-bodied or light-bodied? Think skim milk versus whole milk. Not the taste, obviously, but the weight of it in your mouth.

Structure: How the components of a wine come together (fruit, sugar, alcohol, tannin) and affect the overall balance of a wine.

Tannin: The "grip" of a wine, determined by how much tannin has been extracted from the grapes (and sometimes oak) into the wine.

BODY: LIGHT-BODIED, MEDIUM-BODIED, OR FULL-BODIED?

Wine is often described in terms of body, specifically being **light-**, **medium-**, or **full-bodied**. A bit like milk: skim being light, low-fat being medium, and whole being full-bodied. But in truth what is full-bodied to you might feel medium-bodied to someone who likes big, robust wines. It's all a matter of individual taste. However, having some sort of guide helps when choosing wine. Here's a body guide.

Light-bodied: A light white wine; an easy-going red wine with soft tannins such as Beaujolais; a light-colored rosé wine; most sparkling wines

Medium-bodied: A fruity white, perhaps with a bit of oak; a weightier red wine, but

still not too heavy on the tannins; a very pink rosé

Full-bodied: A rich, sweet white or a big, oaky white; a rich, spicy red, most likely with oak; a vintage Champagne

FEELING FRUITY

As well as these more technical terms, wine is also described on back labels by the fruit characters they might have. For example, is the wine fruity? If so, is it black fruits or red fruits? Is it citrus or tropical fruit? Is it perhaps more vegetal than fruity, say herby or grassy? It might even be more floral than fruity, something like orange blossom or jasmine? With red wine, you may find fruit but also more woody aromas, or spice such as cinnamon. The combination is endless and fascinating. The problem is, sometimes the label might tell you one thing, but your nose and taste buds find another. That's fine, don't get too stuck on what you "should" be finding in your glass. Just enjoy it for what you find. Often, I've got my nose in a glass and there's something I can smell but I just can't put my finger on it. Then the second someone says what it is, it's almost as if I can smell it even more. Equally, when a label tells me I'm going to find licorice in a wine I approach with caution (I can't bear licorice). Luckily, most of the time in wine it's more of a whiff, a trace of licorice rather than a taste.

Take This Down

I live my life by lists. This is for a number of reasons, mostly because with every child that I've had, I seem to have lost the capacity to remember stuff. I wouldn't even contemplate going into a market nowadays without a scribbled list of what I need.

I have learned to scribble down just a few words that will trigger a memory about a wine. A few key pointers—bright, vibrant, juicy, crisp—that will remind me if I liked it or not. Here are some of my notes from a wine competition I took part in recently, just to give you an idea of the sort of pointers I use when tasting professionally.

Unidentified Italian Fiano (white): Clean, fresh nose, with lemon peel notes. Crisp and fresh on the palate, nicely balanced fruit and acidity, hit of citrus fruit on the finish.

Unidentified Australian Grenache (red): Clean, vibrant red currant aromas, bright and juicy with fleshy red fruits on the palate. Medium-weight with well-structured tannins, integrated oak, and kick of spice on the finish.

Not the most exciting tasting notes and certainly not back-label friendly, as they don't tell you anything about where the wine came from and who made it, but when tasting professionally my job is to assess the balance of the wines, to see if they work. When writing tasting notes for wine is your day job, it doesn't feel remotely strange doing this, but if you've never written a tasting note in your life, you probably won't know where to start. If this is the case, I suggest you begin with the simple star system in this journal: One star is okay, three stars is pretty good, five stars means you'll buy it again. No stars equals thanks but no thanks.

As you get comfortable with rating a wine (and remember, no one but you can say if you like it or not, and if so, how much), then try to note down a few words that describe it. Not just fruit, floral, or vegetal descriptors, but words that describe the style of the wine. Is it fresh? Is it juicy? Is it brooding (by which I mean, is it a smoldering red, all rustic and grrrrrr, a bit of an animal)? Of course, this works only if you're trying new things.

Here are a couple of sample wine-tasting notes done by friends.

A dry, aromatic Hungarian Gewürztraminer (white): "Really quite delicious, very quaffable wine that matches perfectly with spicy food, or indeed, and rather randomly, cheese."

"Not usually a fan of fruity wines but this is very drinkable. Can imagine drinking on a warm, sunny weekend afternoon, in the sun. Not really that dry, smells sweeter than it tastes."

"Yummy, delicious floral-tasting wine that chased away the grumpy taste left by my husband!"

A bold, fruity Argentinian Malbec (red):
"Fruity, brash and upfront, very drinkable party wine."

"Full-bodied, fruity, blackberries, warm, and rich."

"Nice fruity smells, bold first taste, fruity and spicy at the end."

"It's reeeally dark and strong (don't know technical term for that). And there's something fruity—really dark black cherries or . . . and don't laugh . . . blueberries? Although I have been eating blueberries today, so maybe they're just stuck in my teeth. Ha ha."

The point is they're the same wines, different reactions. There is no right or wrong, just say (or write) what you see, smell, and taste. Only you know if you like a wine or not, no matter how special or expensive someone tells you it is. Just scribble that note and concentrate on building your own personal wine experience.

The Shape of Wine to Come

Having just told you to make a brief note about a wine if you are trying it for the first time, I have to tell you about my friend Joe. He knows a lot about wine. His father was a chef, he lived in and around hotels growing up, and he lives and breathes wine. He has an amazing palate. Joe also has an encyclopedic mind; he's the one you want on your pub-quiz team. But what I find really amazing about him is that in all the years I've spent writing tasting notes for wines as part of my job, Joe has never written a single one. This is partly due to that incredible memory of his, but he's also got a very short attention span. Writing endless tasting notes is simply not for him. Consequently, he has developed a skill for remembering wines not just because of how they taste, but because of their shape. I know this sounds a bit contrived, but when you think about it, wine does have form. There are ripe, round wines that fill the whole of the mouth and seduce the taste buds, and there are sharp, angular wines with crisp edges and flavors. He once described a wine as akin to having a piece of LEGO in your mouth, and I knew exactly what he meant. Thinking of these wines as shapes or forms rather than "Does this taste of apples?" is a really good way of looking at it.

What Temperature to Taste Wine?

Often, the back label will tell you to serve a red wine at room temperature and a white wine chilled. However, I'm guessing room temperature in your average grand French château is probably a little cooler than my sitting room. Not that I make a habit of taking the temperature of a wine on serving (although there are plenty of gadgets for sale that do this, usually targeted at those with more money than sense), but as a guide, 64 degrees Fahrenheit is about the warmest you want to drink a red—any warmer and it will feel like soup.

For white, go for about 46 degrees Fahrenheit on sparklers and a little less chilled (about 50 degrees Fahrenheit) for other whites. Too cold and the aromas will struggle to make an impact and the flavors will be muted. Again, use common sense. If a white wine feels too cold, leave it on the side and come back in half an hour. If it's too warm, stick it in the freezer for twenty minutes (set the oven timer so you don't forget it).

With red, go for about 60 degrees Fahrenheit, or even slightly chilled in the summer.

JUST CHILLING

Everyone knows how to look good naked: dim lighting. And the funny thing is, there's a wine equivalent of dim lighting. Namely, chilling. The French have a long tradition of serving some of their lighter red wines, particularly those from Beaujolais, slightly chilled. The reason for doing this is that temperature affects the way wine tastes. Cooler temperatures can make the tannins feel more prominent and the alcohol less so. Hence, lighter-bodied red wines with soft tannins can feel a little more robust if slightly chilled. Just as dim lighting masks imperfections, so does chilling a red wine.

TRUE OR FALSE:

"Legs" on a Glass are a Sign of Quality

I have seen the legs in a glass of wine reduce a man to tears of joy, in a "Will you look at the legs on that?" kind of way. He wasn't talking about the same legs ZZ Top sang about, but the effect is not dissimilar, clearly. What he was talking about is the candlestick driplike effect left as the wine drips down the inside of the glass after it's been given a really good swirl. *Those* legs.

So what do legs on a glass of wine mean? Well, mostly they tell you the wine has got lots of alcohol and sugar in it; port and sweet wines such as Sauternes have really noticeable legs. Most wines, however, don't. Some might leave a fleeting trace on the glass, but again these will be the ones with more sugar and/or alcohol in them. It's not necessarily a guide to quality, more a guide to the type of wine you're about to drink. Another myth debunked. You're welcome.

ABOUT White WINE

*H*ere's a reminder of how white wine is made: Pick grapes, crush, press, ferment, mature (sometimes in oak barrels), bottle. It's largely the same process as for red wine, but with one big difference: The grapes are crushed and pressed before fermentation and the juice is not fermented with the skins (where the color is), unlike red wine, which is fermented with the skins.

As you know, white wine can be so light in color as to look almost like water, and it can also be much darker. And this difference in color is because, although the juice is clear, thicker-skinned grape varieties will have more color in them. The resulting white wine will depend on the grape color and how long the juice is left in contact with the skins once the grapes are crushed. The thing about white wine is that it's more delicate than red. It doesn't have the color or tannins to fall back on; it's more about freshness, fruit, and acidity. Winemakers need to be extra careful about keeping the juice clean and fresh, and away from air so that oxidation of the juice (and after fermentation, the wine) is avoided.

There are a couple of other things worth noting about white wine that we don't worry about so much with red wine. The first is whether the wine goes through a natural process called **malolactic fermentation**. This happens naturally after the first fermentation and it converts the sharper, apple-like acids in the wine (the malo acids) to softer, milk-like acids (lactic acids). The process softens the wine, making it less noticeably acidic, and the winemaker can choose whether he wants this to happen or not. A good example is ripe, almost creamy, buttery Chardonnay wines from Australia; they've usually been through malolactic fermentation.

Another big influencing factor is whether the wine has had any lees contact. Lees is basically sediment, made up of dead yeast and skins that may be left in contact with the wine in the barrel or tank for a short time after fermentation. This adds a certain texture to the wine, giving it an almost breadlike smell. If you can, try a Muscadet Sur Lie from the Loire Valley in France; this will show you what I mean. Made from the Melon de Bourgogne grape, Muscadet is made with or without lees contact. *Sur Lie* is, literally, "on the lees." It can be gorgeous; try it, preferably when it's sunny and you have a huge plate of delicious seafood in front of you.

TRUE OR FALSE:
Screw Caps are Only for Cheap Wine

Screw caps have been around for a long time and were originally associated with cheap and not-so-cheerful wines. A handful of pioneering winemakers from the New World, noticeably New Zealand, started using them back in the 1970s for their smarter wines as an alternative to traditional corks. The reason they wanted an alternative to cork was a chemical compound known as TCA, which is the cause of wines being *corked*. If a wine is described as corked, it doesn't mean there are bits of cork floating in it (if that happens, blame it on the corkscrew, or a poor-quality or very old cork). What it means is that the wine smells odd, which can range from slightly dusty-odd to really horrid damp-dishcloth-odd. However badly it is affected, the wine is not nice to drink. It's caused by a reaction between the wine and the TCA, which sits in the natural cork, and there is no way of knowing if a bottle is affected until it's opened.

At the height of the problem, before screw-capped wines became mainstream, the rate of cork taint was around one in every twelve bottles. Things are very different now, with screw caps being used on all quality levels. As one winemaker put it, using a screw cap meant that their wine would reach the drinker just as they intended: fresh and cork-taint-free. There are some who still screw up their noses at the screw cap, but the majority of wines are still sealed with a natural cork and there seems to be room for both. I'm just relieved we're not using camel dung wrapped in muslin, which is what we did before the Romans started using cork. Progress is impossible without change, as they say.

Rosé-Tinted Glasses

And then there is rosé wine. Made like a white wine, treated by winemakers as a white wine, and treated by us as a joyful thing not to be taken too seriously. Which is good. And bad. The problem is, the cheap, sweet "blush" wine from California and the cheap, sweet stuff in funny-shaped bottles from Portugal has given rosé a bit of a reputation, and I'm not talking quality. In fact, rosé wines have enjoyed something of a winemaking revolution in recent years, when more of us started drinking it and wine producers started making better rosés. Think of the beautiful pale-pink rosé wines from the south of France. Or the lovely jewel-like hot pinks from the Navarra region in Spain, or from Chile or Argentina; so many good pinks to choose from!

Rosé wine is not a joke. Rather, it is a joy. It gets its color from being left in contact with the skins of the grapes for a short time (anywhere from a few hours to a few days), so obviously it needs to be made from grapes with a bit of color on the skins. Because of that skin contact, there is a little bit of tannin as well as color in the resulting wine. Some of the most delicious rosé wines around at the moment are made from the red grape Garnacha (in Spain) or Grenache (in France)—same grape, different name. Grenache is one of the grapes often used in the beautiful pale-pink rosé wines made in Provence, where half the rosé in France comes from. Drink it with a tomato salad drenched in dressing and you'll find happiness, I swear.

There is another method of getting color into rosé, and that is **bleeding**, otherwise known in France, much more romantically I must say, as the **saignée method**. Here, a portion of red grape juice is taken after just a short period in contact with the skins, so there is just a bit of color. You can, if you want to, just add some red wine to white wine and make it pink, but by law you can't do this in France, except in Champagne.

In summary, avoid the sweet stuff (not least because it doesn't really taste of wine) and get aboard the pink train. Oh, the places you'll go!

Back to Whites

Let's have a look at the main white grapes.

CHARDONNAY

A bit like reality TV stars, this grape pops up anywhere and everywhere it can. You can't escape it. It's one of the so-called noble grape varieties. A better class of grape, if you like. I've heard lots of people say that they don't like Chardonnay without realizing that it's the grape behind great white Burgundy wines, including Chablis. I suspect these same people have been left traumatized by an over-oaked

Chardonnay at some point in their lives and therefore haven't returned to it in a hurry. However, the over-oaked Chardonnay style is less common now, thanks to changing tastes and responsive winemaking.

As a grape, it is relatively easy to grow and ripen, producing sizeable crops. The actual taste of the grape is pretty nondescript, but winemakers love the malleable character of Chardonnay. They can really play around and influence the end result with their winemaking trickery/alchemy.

Chardonnay loves oak, and it changes character again when allowed to go through the natural **"second" malolactic fermentation process** (which you now know about). It may be ubiquitous, but Chardonnay comes in so many guises that there are enough differing styles to suit different tastes. It is also the white grape variety used to make Champagne (but you already knew that). Whether you want tropical fruit flavors, a peachy queen, a steely Chablis-style wine, or even one with sparkles, there will be a Chardonnay for you. I've just got to help you find it.

CHENIN BLANC
Alas, poor Chenin. It really is a good grape, making some of the finest sweet and dry wines in France, namely from the Loire Valley. However, the same variety is behind some of the cheapest and not-so-cheerful wines from other countries, including South Africa. Treated with love and care, Chenin Blanc can produce beautiful wines with rich lemon flavors and an almost honey-like character. When South Africa does it well, it does it brilliantly. Unloved, it can produce white wines that make one's mouth resemble a cat's backside. Not a good look, even by candlelight. Tread carefully and spend a little more than you would normally, and you'll probably be treated to everything that's good about Chenin. Pick up a bargain Chenin, and, well . . . don't say I didn't warn you.

GEWÜRZTRAMINER
A suitably fitting name for what is a mouthful of a wine. Gewürztraminer is a white grape often described as spicy, and as such, fittingly, it matches up to gently spicy foods like Asian curries. Gewürz (as it's affectionately known by people who have pet names for grapes) is a spicy, floral number, and drinking it is not unlike drinking Turkish delight–scented wine. Odd but delicious. It's one I'm not always in the mood for; but when I am, I always wonder why I don't drink it more often. Not easy to quaff; it's a meal in a glass. Alsace in France is a great place to start your Gewürztraminer journey, with stop-offs in Chile and New Zealand.

PINOT GRIGIO

This one first appeared in inexpensive, brightly lit pizza joints but soon spread from restaurant wine lists onto supermarket shelves and is now one of the best-selling grape varieties we have. Italy is where much of it is grown, but given the success it's had, it's now found in almost every wine-growing country. So, what does it taste like? Well, not an awful lot usually, but it does have an attractive quality: quaffability.

Actually, I am being unfair. Try a Pinot Gris (same grape family) made in the Alsace region in France and all of a sudden there is much more happening in the glass. The same goes for one from Australia, or even New Zealand. Sadly, there'll be much less left in your wallet compared with the cheap-as-chips PG largely found in Italy, but at least you're likely to remember it long after you've forgotten the name of that cheap Italian one you bought on sale last week.

RIESLING

I curtsy to a so-called noble grape variety here. Say "Riesling" to people who take wine far too seriously and you'll see them go misty-eyed. Why the fuss? I have seen the word *ethereal* attached to it, but that's a cop-out. It's difficult to describe, but it goes something like this: lime fruit, mouth-watering acidity, floral notes, a hint of kerosene. Yes, I know I just described a wine as tasting like petroleum, but as ever,

stick some in your mouth, swish it about, suck in some air, and swallow. Then think about what you can taste.

Germany is where you'll find some of the best Riesling wines in the world, but it's also where you'll find some of the worst. Go for the smarter stuff and you'll find that kerosene note. Perhaps I'll go with "ethereal" after all.

SAUVIGNON BLANC

I always think of Sauvignon Blanc as being a rather uptight grape. Basically, if any grape needed a drink, this one does. It's lean, linear, and the grape used to make Sancerre, so I know it can do posh. But sometimes it tries too hard. Think of New Zealand Sauvignon Blanc: more passion fruit than the nipped-in-at-the-waist, Sancerre-style Sauvignons. That's more my style, in fact. Sauvignon Blanc used to fall into the floral—or herbaceous—category of descriptors, but styles are now more varied than ever. Nevertheless, if I stuck my nose into a glass and didn't get a hint of grass/lime/passion fruit, I would feel cheated.

SÉMILLON

I don't often reach for the Sémillon over the others. It's a funny beast—fruity but a little oily. Maybe that's why I can't get excited about it as a single grape variety. Australia's Hunter Valley produces some wonderful Sémillon wines, but you've got to allow them time to develop, and we're not very good at doing that any more. The longest a bottle of wine stays in our kitchen cupboard is a matter of weeks (unless it's been won in a school raffle, then it can stay there for years).

No, where this grape hits its stride is when it's left to rot—actually, properly rot—on the vine, way past when everything else has been picked, and is used to make a sweet wine. Here, you don't want to stop the rot, or **Botrytis cinerea** to give it its proper name, because the juice left in the shriveled grape is so concentrated and sweet, packed with natural sugars, as to be bacchanalian nectar.

Sémillon is one of the grapes—the others are Sauvignon Blanc and Muscadet—used in the making of Bordeaux's great sweet white, Sauternes. In Sauternes, one vine might produce as little as one small bottle of wine. Liquid gold.

TORRONTÉS

This is a grape to watch. It's currently Argentina's calling card, if there is such a thing in white wine, and is making a mark thanks to its light, flowery aromas and easy citrus flavors. It's not expensive to produce, but it must be imbibed young in order to get that lovely freshness. Once it starts to develop in the bottle, it can lose that gorgeous fruit that makes it so delicious. You want this young and fresh.

VIOGNIER

Viognier is a grape with attitude. It carries weight, produces wine with a fairly high alcohol content, and packs a flavor punch. Mostly peach, sometimes orange, occasionally lemons; it's an overflowing fruit bowl. It is most famous as the white grape of the Rhône region and is often added to some of the great northern Rhône red wines (made from the Syrah grape) in dashlike proportions. I love it; it always feels round and ripe to me, like a rather lovely cuddle. It is usually fairly high in alcohol, too, so make that a bear hug.

These are the classic, and a few not-so-classic, ones that make up our patchwork quilt of grape varieties. But look beyond the grape varieties and take note of the following white-wine styles. Make an effort to seek some of these out when you're in the supermarket or local wine shop (not corner shop, unless a big wine range is their speciality) or shopping online. The point is to get off the beaten track without being put off by not really knowing what you're letting yourself in for. Go forage.

SPANISH WHITES AND ROSÉS
(There Is Life Outside Rioja)

If you like clean, crisp, lemony whites, then you have to try an Albariño white. Albariño is a grape grown in the Rias Baixas region in northwest Spain and is very much flavor of the month when it comes to Spanish white wine. Lean and green, with lime fruit and almost ear-splitting acidity, this is a gorgeous spring/summer wine. Some find it too sharp (the Husband included), but happily that means more for me. Navarra is another region to look out for and is a pretty sure bet when looking for a bright, juicy, modern style of rosé. It's not a shy wine, full-bodied by rosé standards.

SOUTHERN FRENCH WHITES
(There Is Life Beyond Chablis)

The grape to look for here is Picpoul, meaning "lip-stinger," apparently because of the high acidity of the grape. I promise you it doesn't sting. It does tingle, though. A good one will give you jasmine-scented aromas, peachlike fruit flavors, and crisp acidity. Coteaux du Languedoc is the region to go for on the label. Another one to look for is Vermentino (the grape) from the Languedoc-Roussillon region. I think young Vermentino, also found in Italy, is what we'd be better off drinking instead of Pinot Grigio, if only we could find it. Sadly, you have to hunt for it. It's lemon-fresh and is exactly right for pasta and pesto.

ITALIAN WHITES MADE FROM UNPRONOUNCEABLE GRAPES

Although it sounds like it, Falanghina is not a sexual act. Rather, it is a grape I told you to put on your fridge-door white list, back when you were getting started (see page 14). You say it like this: Falan-GEEN-ah with a hard "g." Made in southern Italy, largely in Campania, this is one of many brilliantly fresh and relatively uncomplicated Italian whites that can thrill with their simplicity and make you want to eat more. Another two to add to the list are the richer, riper Fiano (that's the name of the grape, also found in southern Italy) and the crisp, applelike Greco di Tufo. (Greco is the grape; Tufo, in Campania, is where it's made.)

CHILEAN WHITES FROM THE CASABLANCA VALLEY AND BEYOND

I absolutely love Chilean wines. When I started buying wine, Chile was all about Chardonnay and Cabernet Sauvignon grown in the huge Central Valley region. Then came the discovery of the Casablanca Valley wines, particularly Sauvignon Blanc. This northern region is generally cooler, with soils and sea breezes suited to ripening aromatic grapes like Sauvignon Blanc and Pinot Noir. Just south of the Casablanca Valley is the San Antonio Valley, another one to watch. Leyda is a region within San Antonio, and the producers there are making some brilliant Sauvignon Blanc wines, crisp as a classic white shirt. Put it on your list of must-haves.

NEW ZEALAND WHITES NOT FROM MARLBOROUGH

Yes, Marlborough Sauvignon Blanc can be lovely, really lovely. But it can also be *everywhere*, stopping you getting beyond it to anything else. So walk past the Marlborough Sauvignons and instead search out the Sauvignon Blancs, Rieslings, and even Gewürztraminers from the Martinborough region, east of Wellington in New Zealand's North Island. Having tasted hundreds of wines from here, all blind (as in the bottles were covered so I didn't know what they were), at an international wine competition, I can tell you that these were the ones that lit up my taste buds. They've got eye-wateringly good Pinot Noir, too.

Once you know what you like, try something different, with confidence:

IF YOU LIKE	THEN TRY	HERE'S WHY
Fruity	Chardonnay, Marsanne, or Roussanne	Same warm peachy fruit, but the grape varieties are less well known.
Not-too-fruity	Chardonnay	Cortese from Italy Gavi, for example, is just one Italian dry white that does fresh fruit but not in an overt way.
Sauvignon Blanc	Rueda from Spain	Light, lemony, and refreshingly different. Rueda is the region, so look for this on the label. Verdejo is the grape.
Pinot Grigio	Falanghina, Cortese, Fiano	Because Pinot Grigio is fine, but there are so many delicious Italian whites to try.
Riesling	Pinot Gris from New Zealand	If you like Riesling, then you might not want to change at all. But if you do, try a Pinot Gris (same grape as Pinot Grigio, but more French in style). Classically beautiful.

THE BOOK CLUB
WINE COURSE

With so many different grapes, countries, and tastes to remember, it's sometimes useful to attach a specific characteristic to a particular flavor in order to give the memory a nudge in the right direction. Funnily enough, I find a handsome leading man often springs to mind: Benicio for Barolo (dark, brooding), Clooney for modern Riojas (gets increasingly better with age). As for Don Draper, he would have to be a Chilean Merlot: smooth but not quite what it seems (for years they thought Chilean Merlot was actually another grape altogether, Carménère. Over time, he/it has been exposed for what he/it really is). Here I give you grapes by literary genre. Depending on what you're in the mood for, there's a grape to match it.

GENRE	GRAPE	NOTES
Bodice Ripper	Gewürztraminer	A white grape. Floral with a bit of spice.
Crime	Malbec	A red grape. Dark, broody, and a little bit dangerous.
Fantasy	Chardonnay	A white grape. Can morph into many things, depending on what the winemaker wants to create.
Historical	Muscat	The world's oldest grape variety. Can make dry whites or sweet whites as well as sparkling wines.
Horror	Pinotage	A red grape grown in South Africa. Not for the faint-hearted.
Literary Prizewinner	Riesling	The ethereal grape. Sometimes difficult to get your head around.
Poetry	Pinot Noir	A red grape, smooth and silky. Beautiful when good, can bring tears to the eyes.
Politics	Sémillon	A white grape. Sometimes fruity, sometimes oily (like politicians).
Romance, light	Torrontés	A grape from Argentina. Fresh, light, and floral.
Romance, dark	Cabernet Sauvignon	A red grape. Black fruits, sometimes spicy.
Sci-Fi	Pinot Grigio	Actually, technically a black grape, not white. (The skin, that is.)

When it comes to tasting and talking about wine, book club is an ideal, informal setting in which to do it. But sometimes it's worth doing it properly, with more than a few wines in front of you so that you can really compare and contrast different styles of wine. Taste a Sauvignon Blanc next to a Chardonnay; or a New World Chardonnay next to a wine from Chablis (also made from the Chardonnay grape, but the latter is normally unoaked). Try a Rioja next to an unoaked red to see what oak does to a wine, or a Prosecco next to a Champagne to compare what bubbles in a bottle do when made in different ways from different countries, with different grapes and different resulting sweetness. But even if you only have one wine in front of you, make time to taste it.

When you are tasting wines side by side like this, it really is worth having a couple of empty glasses in front of you. That way you can pour one, try it, pour another and compare it. By trying wines side by side, you can really stick your nose in, work the taste buds, and see the differences in the wines. We so rarely do this, as most of us only have one glass of wine on the go at any time. Anyway, more than one glass if possible, and even better, a blank sheet of white paper so that you can look at the color of the wine against a white background. At book club, we'll have a few wines on the go and usually share glasses, but when I'm doing wine tastings for people choosing what to serve at a big party, we'll usually taste up to eight wines side by side, so the best wine can win. They will be tasted blind (as in, the bottles are covered up so those choosing don't know which wine is which), and I've learned from experience to number the glasses so as to avoid confusion and delay. Doing it "blind" means that price and place do not affect judgment, so you are really left to concentrate on the smells, tastes, and flavor. And there is nearly always a clear winner, often not the cheapest but rarely the most expensive either.

The Progressive Wine Course

One idea is to organize your book club to bring different wines to each meeting and to do comparative tastings each time you meet, tasting different wines side by side so that you can really see the differences. You don't need to bring a bottle each, obviously, so you could take turns and spread the cost. Here's a suggested running order.

MEETING 1: BUBBLY
○ Bottle of Prosecco
○ Bottle of Champagne
Compare the bubbles, the aromas, and the flavors. See who prefers the softer, sweeter Prosecco style to the crisper, more complex Champagne style.

MEETING 2: SAUVIGNON BLANC
○ Bottle of New Zealand Sauvignon Blanc
○ Bottle of Sancerre
Same grape, different countries. Notice how much the place impacts the flavor of the grape.

MEETING 3: CHARDONNAY
○ Bottle of Australian Chardonnay
○ Bottle of Chablis
Same grape, different countries. Again, see how much place, and winemaking, impacts the flavor.

MEETING 4: OFF-ROAD WHITES
○ Bottle of Argentinian Torrontés
○ Bottle of Chilean Viognier
○ Bottle of German dry Riesling
And now for something completely different. Just look at how exciting life beyond Chardonnay, Sauvignon, and Pinot Grigio can be!

MEETING 5: JUICY REDS
○ Bottle of Beaujolais Villages
   (it will be made from the Gamay grape)
○ Bottle of Chilean Merlot
This one is all about juicy fruit and soft tannins. Again, contrast Old World with New and different grape varieties.

MEETING 6: SPICY REDS
○ Bottle of French Syrah (from the Rhône, a
   blend if necessary)
○ Bottle of South African Pinotage
Again, different countries and different grapes, but feel the tannins at work here. Warning: You'll need food with flavor for this one, something like a chili or spicy stew.

This is only an introduction, but with a bit of forward planning you could bring so many different regions and grape varieties to the table. Just don't forget to talk about the book you've all been reading (and, in my case, have often not quite finished) at some point.

ABOUT *Red* WINE

I love winter. In fact, I have the opposite of seasonal affective disorder. In winter I am happy for the following reasons: (1) I can wear big sweaters. (2) I don't have to depilate (such an odd word) for months. (3) The weekend papers aren't full of endless articles about "festival wear." (4) We can all put in more TV hours (children and grown-ups alike). (5) I love a salad, but not as much as a big plate of beef stew. (6) I can drink more red wine.

If it's cold outside, you're warm inside and you have a gorgeous glass of red in front of you. In fact, it goes hand in hand with curling up and, a bit like hedgehogs, loading up on the food and drink to last us through until the weather gets warmer and the days lighter. There is a heartiness about red wine that white wine just doesn't have.

As you know, the red winemaking process goes like this: Pick grapes, crush, ferment, press, mature (in oak barrels), and bottle.

More than Simply Red

Unlike white wine, red wine has masses of color and tannin. And because all the different grape varieties differ slightly in original color, size, and thickness of skin, calling it simply "red" wine is a bit like calling all shoes "shoes"—from Louboutins to FitFlops—when, as we know, there's a huge difference. Red wine is actually purple, garnet, inky black, light red, dark red, ruby red, maroon—all colors on the red spectrum. Now you just have to choose which red wine you want to snuggle up with. As mentioned, there are thousands of varieties, styles, and places to choose from, but we're going to start with a bunch of grapes that you need to know about.

CABERNET SAUVIGNON

This is the biggie: Like most grape varieties nowadays, this can be found everywhere, but it is as the backbone grape of the Bordeaux region that Cabernet Sauvignon has the right to feel important. In Bordeaux it is almost always blended with other red grapes, including Merlot and Cabernet Franc, but in many Southern Hemisphere countries, including Chile, it is made as a single-variety wine. Almost every bottle containing Cabernet Sauvignon will have "black currant" somewhere on the back label, but as a description, that doesn't begin to cover it. You'll often find all sorts of black fruits in there, such as plums, cherries, or berries. There is something rather stand-offish about Cabernet Sauvignon, just because it knows how good it is. But it is often better blended with other red grapes to make it just a bit softer and more drinkable.

MALBEC

Argentina is making all the noise about Malbec, but it's also the grape behind Cahors in France, many a vacationer's discovery. It is also one of the permitted red grapes grown in Bordeaux, but much of it has been replaced with the more fashionable Cabernet Sauvignon or Merlot grapes. So how to define Malbec? A gate-crasher: late to the party but guaranteed to liven things up. It shakes the taste buds from their noble red grape slumber and says, "LOOK AT ME! I AM MALBEC AND I. AM. GREAT." I do love it, but you have to be in the mood for shouty wine.

MERLOT

Merlot is a really good grape to have around. On its own, it can produce something gorgeous, but it's usually when it's teamed up with a partner, particularly Cabernet Sauvignon, that it really sings. The fleshy character of Merlot complements the harder backbone of Cabernet Sauvignon, and sometimes the sum is indeed better than the parts. Widely planted across most wine-producing countries, this is fairly easy to grow, ripen, and make. It produces soft, lovable wines, hence its popularity the world over.

PINOT NOIR

This is a beauty of a grape to drink once it has been made into wine. However, almost as a reminder that she's in charge, Mother Nature ensures that it's not always easy to grow. Pinot Noir vines don't produce abundant crops, as the thin-skinned grapes can't bear cold weather, rain, or too much heat (fussy little things).

This grape, which originally comes from Burgundy in France, is responsible for the great wines of the Côte d'Or. It's also shaking its tail feathers in New Zealand nowadays, particularly in the South Island in a region called Central Otago. Germany is also raising eyebrows in the wine world with the quality of its Pinot Noir. Rarely cheap but usually good, this is a grape variety to fall in love with over time.

SHIRAZ

So-called in Australia, known as Syrah in France, this is a punchy red grape that gives good fruit. The great red wines of the Rhône Valley are made from Syrah and often described as rich and peppery. I get that, but you can add chocolate to the list, too. When chocolate is used in a tasting note, it doesn't mean actual chocolate, obviously. Rather, it means that the aromas might smell a bit like chocolate. Australia's Barossa Valley has made a mark with its Shiraz wines, bold and beautiful with lots of flavor, tannin and alcohol. Not for the fainthearted, this one.

TEMPRANILLO

This red grape is the key ingredient for Rioja wines. It's a great little grape, producing gorgeous cherry-flavored wines. On its own, the wine can be light, fruity, and fresh but ultimately forgettable. But put it in an oak barrel and things really start to get interesting. In Rioja, the wines are often aged in American oak barrels, imparting a sweet, vanilla-like flavor to the wine. However, lots of producers are now using French oak barrels, making a more restrained but ultimately richer style of wine.

ZINFANDEL

California put Zinfandel on the map, but not as a red wine alone. Vast amounts of sweet white wine made from Zinfandel and called "Blush" is always found in the kitchen at parties at 2 a.m. when everything else has gone. In its red incarnation, Zinfandel makes a big red wine, with lots of flavor and alcohol. In Italy, Zinfandel's relative is called Primitivo and produces a similar style, but a little more rustic and with the sound turned down—definitely one to try if you haven't already.

I could tell you that these are some of the main grape varieties and you should learn them by heart, but (a) I can't think of a good acronym for them and (b) all we've done here is have a look at some of the most commonly found-on-our-shelves grapes.

Now have a look at a handful of fireside-friendly wine styles from different places. They soothe the soul on a cold winter's night, especially if served with a mighty dish of stew. Even better, they are usually properly good value, as they aren't the obvious big names. These are my hidden gems, not always easy to find, but if you ask/do a quick bit of research online you will find them, I promise. And it is absolutely worth the effort. All the wines I describe next are winter-food friendly. In fact, they taste much better with food than without.

SOUTHERN ITALIAN REDS FROM THE PUGLIA REGION

Look for wines made from the Primitivo, Negroamaro, or Malvasia grapes (found in Salice Salentino wines from Puglia). These are all warm, black, fruit-loaded reds with alcohol levels that let you know they are there. They'll make you want to eat sausage and mashed potatoes and watch a boxed set.

SOUTHERN FRENCH REDS FROM THE LANGUEDOC REGION.

This is a region rich with fireside-friendly red wines. My favorites are almost always a blend of red grapes, including Grenache, Syrah, and Mourvèdre, rather than made from one single grape variety. Look out for wines from La Livinière, a subregion in Minervois. Otherwise, look for Côteaux du Languedoc on the front label. These wines are great with slow-cooked stews, especially coq au vin or beef, lamb, or just a simple mushroom risotto.

SPANISH REDS FROM OFF-THE-BEATEN-TRACK REGIONS

Yes, there's Rioja. And I love a good Rioja. But go off the beaten track, east in fact, to a region called Yecla. Here, the wines are made from a red grape called Monastrell. Bright, juicy, and capable of warming even the coldest cockles. Or there's the region of Bierzo, in northwest Spain, where the Mencia grape produces wines with real personality (intense, dark, fruit-laden little beasties). These wines are brilliant with a spicy chorizo and chicken Spanish stew or a simple tomato-based pasta dish with a bit of spice.

TRUE OR FALSE:

Wine is Getting More Alcoholic

Yes, wine has become more alcoholic, specifically New World wines, where the warmer climates produce wines with lots of fruit and lots of alcohol. Natural sugar levels rise as the grapes ripen, so in hotter countries, where the grapes are super-ripe, the resulting wines will be higher in alcohol than in countries with cooler climates. It's also a fashionable thing: big wines with lots of flavor (i.e., alcohol, fruit, and oak) stand out. They're show wines, in other words. They get noticed for their big flavors and get a big score from wine critics. However, the tide is very definitely turning and we're now moving back from these big alcoholic styles of wine to something more subtle and less in-your-face. I want something I can still enjoy on my second glass, rather than feeling like I have to have a lie-down in a darkened room between top-ups. Avoid the 14.5 percent wines and go for something closer to 12 percent. If you want lower still, look to wines from Germany, northern France, or other cooler wine-producing areas.

CHILEAN REDS FROM THE MAULE REGION

You'll find all the big hitters in this region in Chile's Central Valley: Cabernet Sauvignon, Merlot, Shiraz, Pinot Noir. But there's also other stuff to try, including Carignan and Cabernet Franc. Underrated and so often good value, these wines are rich, smooth and, above all, warming. Put a Chilean Cabernet with chili, Shiraz with steak, and Pinot Noir with stuffed peppers.

AUSTRALIAN REDS FROM THE YARRA VALLEY REGION

This is a cool-climate region in Victoria, Australia, and one that has a reputation for producing tear-inducing Pinot Noir wines. Not because of the price, as many red Burgundies do, but because of their standout quality. They are lighter in style than Pinot from other regions in Australia, and more perfumed, but that makes them versatile, especially when it comes to food. Try Yarra Pinot with scallops and bacon, definitely worth a go.

ARGENTINIAN REDS FROM THE MENDOZA REGION

Look for cooler-climate names on the front label, including Luján de Cuyo, where there are Malbecs, Cabernet Sauvignons, and even great Tempranillo wines to choose from. By law, you have to put these with a steak. Fries, too, of course.

Just as you did with white wine, you're probably beginning to know what you like. Now try something else.

IF YOU LIKE	THEN TRY	HERE'S WHY
Cabernet Sauvignon	Malbec from Argentina	Big, bold, and just a little warmer in style. Will make you want to dance.
Merlot	Grenache (probably blended with Syrah and Mouvèdre) from the south of France	Same soft red fruits with added sunshine and oomph. Here, the sum is very definitely greater than the parts.
Shiraz	Syrah from the northern Rhône Valley	Tends to have a sort of "coolness," both in terms of climate and in the style of the wine. Not so shouty, but lots to shout about.
Tempranillo (from Rioja)	Tempranillo from Ribero del Duero	You're still in Spain, just trying something different.

WINE FOR GRILLING

When the weather is hot, hot, hot, chunky reds don't cut it, at least not until there's a plate of barbecued meat on the table. Pre-meat, I usually want something white or pink, possibly with bubbles, and with slightly lower alcohol levels. I'm not talking about the lower-alcohol wines, but the ones made from grapes that produce wines of around 12 percent alcohol or lower naturally.

MOSCATO

This is a catchall name for slightly sweet, lightly fizzy, pink or white wine made from the Muscat grape. Some are frothy, fun, and fit-for-purpose but they are often just as forgettable. If you want to try something really delicious, then Moscato d'Asti with the DOCG stamp (telling you it's from a recognized top-quality region in Italy) is the one to go for. This is one to drink before food. Honestly, the best way to describe it is grapey. Freshly crushed grapes, in fact. And the alcohol is around 5.5 percent, so it's nice and light.

MUSCADET

Made from the Melon de Bourgogne grape in the Loire Valley, France, these wines are often underrated and forgotten about. The good ones are light, fresh, lemony, and really refreshing, and they won't be more than 12 percent alcohol.

RIESLING

There are some gorgeous dry and off-dry German Rieslings that come in at about 8 percent, neatly falling into my naturally lighter wine category. Find one from the Mosel region and you'll probably find a wine with finely balanced lime fruit and sharp acidity, sometimes set off with a bit of sweetness. If you're confused by the label and want a dry or off-dry Riesling (and German wine labels are among the most confusing) then look out for the words *trocken* (meaning dry) or *kabinett*.

VINHO VERDE

Sadly, the Portuguese white wines carrying this name are a bit difficult to find nowadays, but they're worth seeking out. Vinho Verde means "green wine," but this doesn't refer to the color, rather to the fact that the wine is best quaffed young, while it's still loaded with lemon fruit and a gentle natural spritz. Alcohol levels vary but are usually around 9 percent.

REDS

Most red wines are between 12 and 14 percent, and as our global taste for softer, riper styles of wine has grown, so too have the number of wines with alcohol levels nearer 14 than 12 percent. If you want to seek out reds with alcohol levels nearer 12 percent, think cool, as in climate. Look to the Loire Valley in northern France, where some of the red wines (made from the Cabernet Franc grape) are naturally lower in alcohol.

Great Grilling-Friendly Wines

Different dishes call for different wines. Obviously the food will have that char-broiled taste to it, so the wines need to be able to cope with that. But it's as much about the marinades as it is about the cooking, as this will affect the end flavor, particularly if it's a spicy or mustard-based marinade. Here's a quick guide to what wine works well with grilled foods.

THE FOOD	THE WINE	WHY
Burgers	Californian or French Syrah, South Africa Pinotage, California Zinfandel or Malbec	Big flavors—especially if you top the burger with cheese and/or bacon—need a wine with guts. These ones are willing to have a go.
Grilled Vegetables	Provence or Spanish rosé	Has enough weight to cope with charcoal flavors and enough acidity to keep the tastes fresh.
Lamb	Spanish red or southern Italian red	You need soft, juicy warm reds for the lamb. These ones are ideal.
Pork Chops	Gamay (including Beaujolais Villages) or Grenache	Pork is lighter in flavor (unless you've covered it in a mustard marinade), so the bright flavors of Gamay or Grenache are a great fit.
Salmon Kebabs	Sauvignon Blanc, if herby or dry; Riesling, if chile-flecked or young; Pinot Noir, if really spicy	You need a wine with acidity and freshness here, something that won't dominate the fish.
Sausages	Southern French red or Spanish Tempranillo	You need something with fruit but not too much tannin, as it will clash with the fat in the sausages.
Spicy Chicken Drumsticks	Chardonnay with a bit of oak or a Viognier	Yes, you can go for whites with grilled meats, but they need lots of flavor if they're going to be heard over the flavors of the food.
Steaks	Argentinian Malbec	An obvious bedfellow for the steak because of its weight, but Carménère can do the job, too.

MATCHING

Food

AND *Wine*

*T*here are lots of unofficial "rules" when it comes to matching food with wine, the most obvious one being red wine with meat, white wine with fish. I happen to think that's not strictly true. If you are going to remember just one rule about matching food and wine, make it this one: Think about the weight of flavor of the food and try to match it with a wine of a similar weight.

Here, weight refers to the body and fullness of the wine. This, of course, means there are endless possible combinations and some will work better than others. There is also the question of whether a wine needs food at all. I say yes it does, to make it taste better and to avoid getting a hangover. So, you've got your one simple rule memorized—match the weight of the dish to the weight of the wine—and here's how you do that: First of all, think about how the dish in question is cooked, and what it's cooked with. The wine needs to be able to cope with the dominant flavor of the dish. How it is cooked—steamed, grilled, fried, or roasted, or even raw in a salad—calls for wines of different weight. Know this and you have a better chance of matching your dish with a wine that will complement rather than dominate the food. You want to be able to taste both food and wine, not just one or the other.

Before we look at actual ingredients, we need to understand what it is about wine that affects tastes.

Acidity: In wine, acidity helps to cut through oily, creamy, or salty food. Oily fish needs wine with "bite."

Body: The golden rule is to match the body—the weight—of the wine to the weight of the dish. A big beef stew will suffocate a delicate, light white wine, while a spicy Côtes du Rhône will shout down a beautifully delicate fish dish.

Oak: In wine, oak adds weight and complexity, so it calls for a dish with oomph. That beef stew will do nicely.

Sweetness: Natural sweetness in a wine is fantastic when it matches sweetness in a dish.

Tannin: Here's another science bit. The tannins in red wine help break down the protein and fat in (mostly red) meats.

Let's put these basics into practice and have a look at specific ingredients.

CHEESE
Lots of different types of cheese work best with different styles of wine, but again, a few guidelines are blue with sweet (think Stilton and Sauternes or port) and hard-flavored cheese with bigger reds (the big-hitting Italian Amarone is one to try). Soft cheese likes aromatic whites. Again, one of nature's party tricks is to create a cheese somewhere and then ensure the local wine is an almost unbeatable match. If you haven't tried the goats' cheese from Chavignol with a white wine from Sancerre, may I suggest you do? Add it to your bucket list. Sometimes I go for just one type of strong cheese—albeit a fairly big hunk—and have a bottle of fruity red in the wings. No one has complained yet.

CHICKEN AND OTHER BIRDS
As you now know, it's as much about the way the chicken is cooked and what it's served with as it is about the actual meat. Simple roast chicken with salad loves a creamy, fruity Chardonnay, with a bit of oak perhaps, but add all the trimmings of a big Sunday roast and you'll find that a smooth medium-bodied red does the trick. If you're having a game bird, go for Pinot Noir.

FISH
Generally speaking, a dry white wine will suit fish more than a red wine will. Chablis, with its steely acidity and (usual) lack of oak makes it a timeless classic for many a simple white fish dish. However, if the fish has got a stronger flavor, such as salmon or tuna, then you can branch into red wine territory. Not a great big tannic beast, but something with soft tannins, Pinot Noir, for example, can work brilliantly. For oily fish such as smoked salmon, something with lots of acidity and "bite" to help cut through the oiliness is the way to go. It's a cliché, but smoked salmon and Champagne is a knockout combination. For sushi lovers, wine with a bit of natural sweetness works; look for something with "late harvest" on the label. If grilled prawns are on the menu, you have to drink Manzanilla.

HERBY FOOD

If you're faced with a plate of food that's absolutely covered in a particular herb, and that herb is going to be the dominant flavor in the dish, you need to find a wine that likes it. Pick a rosé to accompany thyme. Go for a dry Muscat if you're minted (herb-wise, not cash-wise). Basil loves Italian whites, while rosemary prefers a red, especially if served with lamb.

RED MEAT

The fuller flavors of red meat demand fuller flavors from the wine it's going to be eaten with, but there are some things to watch out for. Tannin can clash with fat, so if you've got a fatty piece of meat, avoid very tannic reds. Go for Cabernet Sauvignon over Cabernet Franc, for example. Again, think about the weight of the flavors from the meat—and whatever sauce you've got with it—and try to balance it with a red that will stand up to it but not shout over it.

SPICY FOOD

This is a tricky one, as there are so many varying degrees of spiciness in foods. The really spicy stuff—hotter-than-hot curries for example—leave the taste buds wanting something cool and refreshing with a fairly neutral flavor. Beer will cleanse the palate, but it won't really work with the food. Rather, it turns its back on it. If, however, the food isn't so spicy as to render your taste buds helpless, then wine can have a look in. Asian-influenced food is very happy with a dry or off-dry white wine, especially fruity ones with a good lick of acidity. Gewürztraminer is a case in point, and the literal meaning of *gewürz* is "spice." Made for each other, clearly. Stay away from oaky wines; they don't get along so well with spice. Spicy red meat dishes are better off with a fruity Australian Shiraz, while a drier, more tannic or oaky red is more likely to clash with the spice in the dish.

VEGETABLES

Annoyingly, veggie dishes do present some fairly random challenges when it comes to matching them with the right sort of wines. Tomatoes are relatively high in acidity, so match them with a wine that has the same, such as cooler-climate white wines; Sauvignon Blanc is especially good. Another one is asparagus, which can make some white wines taste almost like tin. Not that I've eaten tin, but hopefully you'll know what I'm driving at, a sort of metallic taste. I rather like Riesling with asparagus, as it happens. Simple salads call for simple white wines. Pinot Grigio works well. An omelette just needs a glass of crisp, dry white wine, such as unoaked Chardonnay (Chablis, for example) or Gavi (an Italian white made from the Cortese grape) or Pinot Gris from Alsace or New Zealand. Believe me, there are endless great combinations.

The Age of a Wine is an Indication of Quality

The age of a wine is not necessarily an indication of quality. Of course, there are lots of wines that are made to be aged and will improve if left to "age" in the bottle. However, the majority of wines made today are made to be consumed within the year, or perhaps within two years if stretching. White wines especially; the younger they are imbibed the better, as the delicate aromas and fruit flavors will develop over time, but not in a good way. In fact, they will lose the best thing about them: their freshness.

Red wines, especially those aged in oak, are made to age and have tannin in their structure, which provides the backbone to allow them to age gracefully, and hopefully develop into a more interesting wine over time. The nightmare is, there is no way of knowing how a wine is ageing in the bottle, apart from cracking it open and drinking it. If you have a case of a particular wine, this isn't a problem; if the wine still tastes too young, too tight, just leave it for a while—another six months, another year—before coming back and trying another bottle. But if you have just the one bottle—bad luck! If you are spending big money on investment wines, they will improve over decades. You'll just have to be patient. And then invite me for dinner.

What Wine When?

Life is too short for lots of things, but especially to drink bad wine. Obviously, you should drink whatever you are in the mood for, it's just that by putting a bit of thought into the matching bit, you can improve a meal no end. And if you are cooking something that requires some effort and time, why not bring out the best in the flavors with a wine that supports the dish rather than works against it? By opening the right bottle midweek, you can perk up even the slackest meal by making the flavors sing rather than mumble. And by putting the right bottles on the table when someone important comes for dinner, you can look ever so knowledgeable (which, having read all this, you now are). The thing is, you need to put it into practice in order to learn from experience. Here are some combinations to try, both classic and not so classic. Write notes in this journal so that you can repeat the successful pairings and avoid the ones you don't like.

DISH	CLASSIC PAIRING	NOT-SO-CLASSIC PAIRING
Burger	Cabernet Sauvignon from anywhere	California Zinfandel
Chicken Curry (mild)	Beer	Champagne (not kidding)
Five-Spice Pork Belly	New Zealand Pinot Noir	New Zealand Chardonnay
Lamb Chops with Herb Butter	Red Bordeaux (Cabernet-Merlot blend)	Argentinian Malbec
Lasagne	Chianti	Southern Italian red (Primitivo, Nero d'Avola)
Mushroom Risotto	Chianti	Chilean Pinot Noir
Simple Salad	Pinot Grigio	Picpoul de Pinet (southern French white)
Thai Fish Curry	Gewürtzraminer from Alsace	Australian Pinot Gris

HOW to *Buy* WINE

I don't want you to have to wing it on buying wine any more. You now know how wine is made. You know why white wine is white, why rosé wine is pink, and why red wine is red. You know what affects how a wine tastes— people, place, and grapes—and you know that when it comes to matching food and wine, you think about the weight of the wine first.

You know about the main grape varieties and you know that sometimes a blend of grapes is more interesting than a single grape variety. You know how to taste wine, and you know how to scribble your thoughts down so that you can remember what you like and don't like. But what you don't know, yet, is how to buy wine with confidence. Let's have a look at how to do that.

Can You Judge a Wine by its Label?

Imagine buying a pair of shoes without trying them on. Oh, most of you have done that. Okay, how about ordering a pizza and asking the waiter to put whatever he wants on it? You wouldn't, unless you are the kind of person who'll risk having to pay for and consume something you might not like, though you won't know that you don't like it until you've tried it, by which time you'll have paid for it and won't be able to get your money back. See where I'm going?

Buying wine can be a game of chance, but it can be made easier by knowing what to look for on the label and how to spot the signs that will point you in the right direction. The first things to look for include where the wine is made and what grape variety, or varieties, it's made from. Unlike wine from the New World, Old World wines often don't have a grape variety stated on the front label. You are supposed to just *know* that Chablis is made from Chardonnay, red Burgundy is made from Pinot

Noir, and Rioja is made from Tempranillo. Luckily, the idea of helping us find what we like has caught on and it's becoming more common to find a reference to the grape somewhere on the back label.

Vintage is another sign. If a wine has a year on it, the wine is made from grapes picked that year, that is, "the vintage." It's telling you the year the harvest happened. Some wine doesn't have a year on it, because it's made from a blend of grapes from different years. Champagne is a good example here, with the letters "**NV**" (standing for non-vintage) shown proudly on the label. Because, in Champagne, blending is an art form and the aim is for each "house" or producer to create a style of wine that doesn't change from year to year for their signature non-vintage blend. So, having a vintage on the label doesn't automatically mean it is better than one without; it depends on the wine.

Wines that do list the vintage, how-ever, are sometimes shouting about their differences from previous years. Port is an example of how vintage is everything. With port, not every year is deemed good enough to be "declared"—meaning the port houses decide whether it's a good enough year to shout about—as a vintage year, hence all the fuss about vintage port. Remember, older doesn't always mean better. If you want a really fresh, crisp, fruity dry white or rosé, then usually the younger, the better. For inexpensive juicy ripe reds, too, youth is good.

As we've already established, one shouldn't judge a book by its cover, but I do think that a good guide is the look of the label. If a wine producer has bothered to have a good-looking label made for their wine, then it shows they're making an effort. Of course, there are exceptions: I have tried bottles with a nice-enough label and found a horror within. Equally, a horrible label might contain a gem of a wine. However, a good rule of thumb is, if they've taken time with the label, they care about what you think.

Your best bet when it comes to labels is to look at the story on the back label. What has the producer decided to tell you? What the wine tastes like? What food to match it with? If there is good information on the back label then, again, the producer (or the shop selling you the wine) is at least making an effort to help you.

Buying Wine in a Supermarket

The general approach seems to be bottom shelf for the cheap stuff, middle shelf for better everyday, and top shelf for special occasions. There is something psychologi-cal in reaching down for cheap and reach-ing up for expensive, while the middle feels safe. Other than that, the chances are you're pretty much on your own. The wine aisle will have at least five times the num-ber of products as the cereal aisle, and the brands are few and far between. If there is a brand on the shelf that you know and love, then you're in luck. But if you want to try something different and expand your wine horizons, it's very difficult to know where to look. For a start, the wines are often stocked on the shelf according to color and country rather than style, leaving you no option but to go cross-country. At this point, look for a signpost. Start with a grape you like and go from there.

So, if you like Pinot Grigio, go to Italy and try a different white, either a blend or a regional wine, but something that tells you it's dry and crisp (look on the back label for a description, or symbol or number describing the wine). If you like French red, go to the region you normally buy from and pick up a bottle from another region instead.

A word on wine deals: The definition of a good wine sale is when it's an offer on something I know, or have at least heard of, and something I quite fancy trying ("need" would be stretching it). I want to feel I'm getting great value—big-name Champagne deals spring to mind. However, half-price for a bottle of something I've never tried before isn't as appealing. In anticipation of would-be bargains, the bottles in supermarkets with dust on them are often the hidden gems on the top shelf. When they are sold through as a bin-end (a name given to the last few remaining bottles of wine from a particular collection, usually sold at a big discount), the dust-covered bottle can be had at a very good price.

Buying in Wine Shops

Generally, people who work in wine shops love wine. Most of them love drinking it, and most of them love talking about it. If you've taken the trouble to go to a wine shop and aren't just buying wine in the supermarket along with the rest of your groceries, then I'm assuming you are in slightly less of a hurry to get in and out. Tell them what you usually drink and ask if they can recommend something similar that you haven't tried before. Experiment, go crazy, be brave. Remember that the range before you will have been put together by someone who's unusually nuts about wine; they will probably have tried every single wine and know the story behind each one.

That's the best bit when choosing a new wine: finding out about who made it, why they made it, and what they say about it. Too often, we don't get to find out the story behind a wine, and yet it's almost always more memorable when we know about the people who made the stuff. A good wine shop will have people who know this and they will love seeing you leave with something you've never tried before only to come back for more. Avoid the bottles with dust on them, though; they've obviously been sitting there a while (which, in a wine shop, isn't a good sign).

Don't buy in quantity unless you have already tried the wine, even if that means buying a bottle one day and returning to stock up the next.

Buying Online

This is a great way to buy wine—from the sofa (brilliant!). It also means you can wander off on a fact-finding thread about a particular wine without having to actually get up. Annoyingly, winery websites are usually a bit dull, with lots of technical information on the wine. Great for insomnia, but not so great for getting us enthused. But that is changing, slowly. The good ones give you a sense of place, tell you about the people behind the wine, and where you can buy it. There is also a raft of online-specific wine retailers worth exploring, including Zachys, Garagiste Wine, Premier Cru, and K&L Wine Merchants. One of the most useful tools is reading what other customers have said about a wine. Obviously, one person's favorite is another's most revolting, but at least it's a signpost of sorts.

Buying Wine in Restaurants

Due to the line of work I am in, I don't often have to fight over the wine list with my restaurant companion, be it the Husband ("You don't have to read the *whole* thing," he likes to say), Mother ("Anything but Chardonnay, unless it's Chablis," she invariably offers), or friend ("Does that come in a big glass?" she will ask, hopefully), but if you aren't usually the one to choose, make sure you become the one

who accepts the wine list first, and don't feel rushed. Experience is all and knowledge is power. Assuming you know what you're going to be eating, choose the color of the wine you're going to have—or at least start with—and work your way down.

House wines are going to be good but probably not memorable albeit a safe bet. But we're getting out of that comfort zone, remember? So, don't always go for the house wine. If you're feeling even slightly flush (you are in a restaurant, after all), then try something new. Not the most expensive stuff—that's there for the dudes trying to impress dates and work colleagues—no, what you need to do is cherry-pick, and having a bit of wine knowledge helps you do just that. There is almost always a bargain to be had on a wine list. You just need to know how to find it. Again, ask questions if the wine server sounds like she knows her stuff. If they are really trying to sell you a particular bottle, ask to try a bit first. If not, buy it by the glass and try out a few different wines around the table.

If you're having a wine that's sold by the glass, it's worth asking how long the bottle has been open—nicely, of course. Sometimes they can be left open for more than a few days, exposing the wine to oxygen that flattens its flavor and taste. You shouldn't be afraid to ask; you are paying for it, after all. When in doubt, go for more recent vintages rather than older vintages, as younger wine is generally less risky.

I realize that I'm pretty well equipped to work my way around the wine maze that is the supermarket shelf, the wine shop, or the restaurant wine list, but because there's so much choice when it comes to wine—a ridiculous amount, really—even I get lost on occasion. I do have to find out what I can from the labels (often not that easy, as we've seen) and then just go with my gut. It's a bit of a lucky dip, except that sometimes it might turn out to be unlucky, in which case, I make a note of it and don't make that mistake again. There *are* pointers—country, region, grape—to help you. You might not win every time, but at least you're trying something different and you might unearth a gem.

THE Last Drop

We've talked about a lot of different styles of wine. These are just ideas, all tried and tested, and aimed to give you a steer if you want some wine inspiration. To find the wines we've covered, simply go to the wine website of the place you shop and type in the grape variety.

See what comes up and find out a bit about the wine before you go and buy it. Of course, if you're buying from your local wine shop, you can ask for help finding them and for specific recommendations. As we've already established, the majority of people who work in wine shops are dying to talk about wine; you just need to ask. And don't get the equivalent of hair-salon paralysis and freeze when asked what you'd like and how much you want to spend. Instead, have a maximum price in mind before you start, tell them what sort of taste and feeling you're looking for (gleaned from reviewing your entries in this journal before you go), and enjoy the process of discovery, one nice bottle a week at a time. There is so much more I could tell you, but what you've got here is the need-to-know stuff. You are ready for the journey, so I'll leave you to it. Here's what I'm hoping we've achieved:

1. You are inspired to try new and different wines, not just stick to what you know.
2. You have a better idea of what to look for when you are standing at the foot of the wall of wine.
3. You will confidently reach for the wine list next time you are eating out and won't just go for the second one down on the list.
4. You have discovered which styles of wine you enjoy most and now understand why you like them.
5. You will keep glasses of forgettable wine consumed to an absolute minimum. And every week you will try at least one new wine and add your tasting notes to this journal. Yes, it might stop you from doing something properly productive and useful, but I do like to think I'm providing an essential service, namely stopping you from drinking uninteresting (or even bad) wine.

Here's to your next glass of very nice wine.

Date tasted . . . .

Okay   Pretty good   Will buy again

The Overview

WINE STYLE . . . . **COUNTRY** . . . .

GRAPE(S) . . . . **PRICE** . . . .

WINEMAKER (OR NAME OF PRODUCER) . . . .

Look, Smell & Taste

COLOR IS . . . .

SMELLS LIKE:

Fruity
- ○ Citrus
- ○ Tropical
- ○ Berry
- ○ Dried fruits

Veggie
- ○ Herby
- ○ Grassy
- ○ Green pepper
- ○ Minty

Bready
- ○ Yeasty

Floral
- ○ Orange blossom
- ○ Jasmine

Spicy
- ○ Pepper
- ○ Cloves
- ○ Cinnamon
- ○ Licorice

Woody
- ○ Smoky
- ○ Oaky
- ○ Vanilla

Earthy
- ○ Old socks
- ○ Musty
- ○ Moldy

Weird
- ○ Eggy
- ○ Burnt match
- ○ Cardboard

TASTES OF . . . .

. . . .

Structure & Balance

THE ZIP (ACIDITY)
○ Low Buzz
○ Medium Bite
○ Lip-Tingling High

THE GRIP (TANNINS)
○ Big
○ Firm
○ Soft

THE OOMPH (BODY)
○ Light-bodied
○ Medium-bodied
○ Full-bodied

Three to five key words that will remind me what this wine was like ....

....

What I ate and how the wine matched ....

....

....

Takeaway tasting notes (look, smell, taste, and balance) ....

....

....

....

....

....

....

....

....

....

Date tasted . . . .

Okay   Pretty good   Will buy again

The Overview

WINE STYLE . . . . **COUNTRY** . . . .

GRAPE(S) . . . . **PRICE** . . . .

WINEMAKER (OR NAME OF PRODUCER) . . . .

Look, Smell & Taste

COLOR IS . . . .

SMELLS LIKE:

Fruity
- ○ Citrus
- ○ Tropical
- ○ Berry
- ○ Dried fruits

Veggie
- ○ Herby
- ○ Grassy
- ○ Green pepper
- ○ Minty

Bready
- ○ Yeasty

Floral
- ○ Orange blossom
- ○ Jasmine

Spicy
- ○ Pepper
- ○ Cloves
- ○ Cinnamon
- ○ Licorice

Woody
- ○ Smoky
- ○ Oaky
- ○ Vanilla

Earthy
- ○ Old socks
- ○ Musty
- ○ Moldy

Weird
- ○ Eggy
- ○ Burnt match
- ○ Cardboard

TASTES OF . . . .

Structure & Balance

THE ZIP (ACIDITY)
- Low Buzz
- Medium Bite
- Lip-Tingling High

THE GRIP (TANNINS)
- Big
- Firm
- Soft

THE OOMPH (BODY)
- Light-bodied
- Medium-bodied
- Full-bodied

Three to five key words that will remind me what this wine was like . . . .

What I ate and how the wine matched . . . .

Takeaway tasting notes (look, smell, taste, and balance) . . . .

Date tasted . . . .

☆ ☆ ☆ ☆ ☆

Okay   Pretty good   Will buy again

The Overview

WINE STYLE . . . . **COUNTRY** . . . .

GRAPE(S) . . . . **PRICE** . . . .

WINEMAKER (OR NAME OF PRODUCER) . . . .

Look, Smell & Taste

COLOR IS . . . .

SMELLS LIKE:

Fruity
- ○ Citrus
- ○ Tropical
- ○ Berry
- ○ Dried fruits

Veggie
- ○ Herby
- ○ Grassy
- ○ Green pepper
- ○ Minty

Bready
- ○ Yeasty

Floral
- ○ Orange blossom
- ○ Jasmine

Spicy
- ○ Pepper
- ○ Cloves
- ○ Cinnamon
- ○ Licorice

Woody
- ○ Smoky
- ○ Oaky
- ○ Vanilla

Earthy
- ○ Old socks
- ○ Musty
- ○ Moldy

Weird
- ○ Eggy
- ○ Burnt match
- ○ Cardboard

TASTES OF . . . .

. . . .

. . . .

Structure & Balance

THE ZIP (ACIDITY)
- Low Buzz
- Medium Bite
- Lip-Tingling High

THE GRIP (TANNINS)
- Big
- Firm
- Soft

THE OOMPH (BODY)
- Light-bodied
- Medium-bodied
- Full-bodied

Three to five key words that will remind me what this wine was like ....

....

What I ate and how the wine matched ....

....

....

Takeaway tasting notes (look, smell, taste, and balance) ....

....

....

....

....

....

....

....

....

....

Date tasted ....

Okay   Pretty good   Will buy again

The Overview

WINE STYLE ....   **COUNTRY** ....

GRAPE(S) ....   **PRICE** ....

WINEMAKER (OR NAME OF PRODUCER) ....

Look, Smell & Taste

COLOR IS ....

SMELLS LIKE:

Fruity
- Citrus
- Tropical
- Berry
- Dried fruits

Veggie
- Herby
- Grassy
- Green pepper
- Minty

Bready
- Yeasty

Floral
- Orange blossom
- Jasmine

Spicy
- Pepper
- Cloves
- Cinnamon
- Licorice

Woody
- Smoky
- Oaky
- Vanilla

Earthy
- Old socks
- Musty
- Moldy

Weird
- Eggy
- Burnt match
- Cardboard

TASTES OF ....

....

....

Structure & Balance

THE ZIP (ACIDITY)
○ Low Buzz
○ Medium Bite
○ Lip-Tingling High

THE GRIP (TANNINS)
○ Big
○ Firm
○ Soft

THE OOMPH (BODY)
○ Light-bodied
○ Medium-bodied
○ Full-bodied

Three to five key words that will remind me what this wine was like

What I ate and how the wine matched

Takeaway tasting notes (look, smell, taste, and balance)

Date tasted ....

Okay   Pretty good   Will buy again

The Overview

WINE STYLE .... **COUNTRY** ....

GRAPE(S) .... **PRICE** ....

WINEMAKER (OR NAME OF PRODUCER) ....

Look, Smell & Taste

COLOR IS ....

SMELLS LIKE:

Fruity
○ Citrus
○ Tropical
○ Berry
○ Dried fruits

Veggie
○ Herby
○ Grassy
○ Green pepper
○ Minty

Bready
○ Yeasty

Floral
○ Orange blossom
○ Jasmine

Spicy
○ Pepper
○ Cloves
○ Cinnamon
○ Licorice

Woody
○ Smoky
○ Oaky
○ Vanilla

Earthy
○ Old socks
○ Musty
○ Moldy

Weird
○ Eggy
○ Burnt match
○ Cardboard

TASTES OF ....
....
....

Structure & Balance

THE ZIP (ACIDITY)
- ○ Low Buzz
- ○ Medium Bite
- ○ Lip-Tingling High

THE GRIP (TANNINS)
- ○ Big
- ○ Firm
- ○ Soft

THE OOMPH (BODY)
- ○ Light-bodied
- ○ Medium-bodied
- ○ Full-bodied

Three to five key words that will remind me what this wine was like

What I ate and how the wine matched

Takeaway tasting notes (look, smell, taste, and balance)

Date tasted . . . .

Okay   Pretty good   Will buy again

The Overview

WINE STYLE . . . .   **COUNTRY** . . . .

GRAPE(S) . . . .   **PRICE** . . . .

WINEMAKER (OR NAME OF PRODUCER) . . . .

Look, Smell & Taste

COLOR IS . . . .

SMELLS LIKE:

Fruity
- ○ Citrus
- ○ Tropical
- ○ Berry
- ○ Dried fruits

Veggie
- ○ Herby
- ○ Grassy
- ○ Green pepper
- ○ Minty

Bready
- ○ Yeasty

Floral
- ○ Orange blossom
- ○ Jasmine

Spicy
- ○ Pepper
- ○ Cloves
- ○ Cinnamon
- ○ Licorice

Woody
- ○ Smoky
- ○ Oaky
- ○ Vanilla

Earthy
- ○ Old socks
- ○ Musty
- ○ Moldy

Weird
- ○ Eggy
- ○ Burnt match
- ○ Cardboard

TASTES OF . . . .

. . . .

. . . .

Structure & Balance

THE ZIP (ACIDITY)
- Low Buzz
- Medium Bite
- Lip-Tingling High

THE GRIP (TANNINS)
- Big
- Firm
- Soft

THE OOMPH (BODY)
- Light-bodied
- Medium-bodied
- Full-bodied

Three to five key words that will remind me what this wine was like ....

....

What I ate and how the wine matched ....

.. ..

....

Takeaway tasting notes (look, smell, taste, and balance) ....

....

....

....

....

....

....

....

The Overview

WINE STYLE . . . .   **COUNTRY** . . . .

GRAPE(S) . . . .   **PRICE** . . . .

WINEMAKER (OR NAME OF PRODUCER) . . . .

Look, Smell & Taste

COLOR IS . . . .

SMELLS LIKE:

Fruity
- ○ Citrus
- ○ Tropical
- ○ Berry
- ○ Dried fruits

Veggie
- ○ Herby
- ○ Grassy
- ○ Green pepper
- ○ Minty

Bready
- ○ Yeasty

Floral
- ○ Orange blossom
- ○ Jasmine

Spicy
- ○ Pepper
- ○ Cloves
- ○ Cinnamon
- ○ Licorice

Woody
- ○ Smoky
- ○ Oaky
- ○ Vanilla

Earthy
- ○ Old socks
- ○ Musty
- ○ Moldy

Weird
- ○ Eggy
- ○ Burnt match
- ○ Cardboard

TASTES OF . . . .

. . . .

. . . .

Structure & Balance

THE ZIP (ACIDITY)
- ○ Low Buzz
- ○ Medium Bite
- ○ Lip-Tingling High

THE GRIP (TANNINS)
- ○ Big
- ○ Firm
- ○ Soft

THE OOMPH (BODY)
- ○ Light-bodied
- ○ Medium-bodied
- ○ Full-bodied

Three to five key words that will remind me what this wine was like ....

....

What I ate and how the wine matched ....

....

....

Takeaway tasting notes (look, smell, taste, and balance) ....

....

....

....

....

....

....

....

....

Date tasted ....

Okay   Pretty good   Will buy again

The Overview

WINE STYLE .... **COUNTRY** ....

GRAPE(S) .... **PRICE** ....

WINEMAKER (OR NAME OF PRODUCER) ....

Look, Smell & Taste

COLOR IS ....

SMELLS LIKE:

Fruity
○ Citrus
○ Tropical
○ Berry
○ Dried fruits

Veggie
○ Herby
○ Grassy
○ Green pepper
○ Minty

Bready
○ Yeasty

Floral
○ Orange blossom
○ Jasmine

Spicy
○ Pepper
○ Cloves
○ Cinnamon
○ Licorice

Woody
○ Smoky
○ Oaky
○ Vanilla

Earthy
○ Old socks
○ Musty
○ Moldy

Weird
○ Eggy
○ Burnt match
○ Cardboard

TASTES OF ....

....

....

Structure & Balance

THE ZIP (ACIDITY)
○ Low Buzz
○ Medium Bite
○ Lip-Tingling High

THE GRIP (TANNINS)
○ Big
○ Firm
○ Soft

THE OOMPH (BODY)
○ Light-bodied
○ Medium-bodied
○ Full-bodied

Three to five key words that will remind me what this wine was like

What I ate and how the wine matched

Takeaway tasting notes (look, smell, taste, and balance)

Date tasted ....

☆ ☆ ☆ ☆ ☆

Okay　　　Pretty good　　Will buy again

The Overview

WINE STYLE .... **COUNTRY** ....

GRAPE(S) .... **PRICE** ....

WINEMAKER (OR NAME OF PRODUCER) ....

Look, Smell & Taste

COLOR IS ....

SMELLS LIKE:

Fruity
○ Citrus
○ Tropical
○ Berry
○ Dried fruits

Veggie
○ Herby
○ Grassy
○ Green pepper
○ Minty

Bready
○ Yeasty

Floral
○ Orange blossom
○ Jasmine

Spicy
○ Pepper
○ Cloves
○ Cinnamon
○ Licorice

Woody
○ Smoky
○ Oaky
○ Vanilla

Earthy
○ Old socks
○ Musty
○ Moldy

Weird
○ Eggy
○ Burnt match
○ Cardboard

TASTES OF ....

....

....

Structure & Balance

THE ZIP (ACIDITY)
- ○ Low Buzz
- ○ Medium Bite
- ○ Lip-Tingling High

THE GRIP (TANNINS)
- ○ Big
- ○ Firm
- ○ Soft

THE OOMPH (BODY)
- ○ Light-bodied
- ○ Medium-bodied
- ○ Full-bodied

Three to five key words that will remind me what this wine was like ....

....

What I ate and how the wine matched ....

....

....

Takeaway tasting notes (look, smell, taste, and balance) ....

....

....

....

....

....

....

....

....

....

Date tasted ....

☆ ☆ ☆ ☆ ☆
Okay   Pretty good   Will buy again

The Overview

WINE STYLE .... **COUNTRY** ....

GRAPE(S) .... **PRICE** ....

WINEMAKER (OR NAME OF PRODUCER) ....

Look, Smell & Taste

COLOR IS ....

SMELLS LIKE:

Fruity
○ Citrus
○ Tropical
○ Berry
○ Dried fruits

Veggie
○ Herby
○ Grassy
○ Green pepper
○ Minty

Bready
○ Yeasty

Floral
○ Orange blossom
○ Jasmine

Spicy
○ Pepper
○ Cloves
○ Cinnamon
○ Licorice

Woody
○ Smoky
○ Oaky
○ Vanilla

Earthy
○ Old socks
○ Musty
○ Moldy

Weird
○ Eggy
○ Burnt match
○ Cardboard

TASTES OF ....
....
....

Structure & Balance

THE ZIP (ACIDITY)
- Low Buzz
- Medium Bite
- Lip-Tingling High

THE GRIP (TANNINS)
- Big
- Firm
- Soft

THE OOMPH (BODY)
- Light-bodied
- Medium-bodied
- Full-bodied

Three to five key words that will remind me what this wine was like

What I ate and how the wine matched

Takeaway tasting notes (look, smell, taste, and balance)

Date tasted . . . .

Okay   Pretty good   Will buy again

The Overview

WINE STYLE . . . .   **COUNTRY** . . . .

GRAPE(S) . . . .   **PRICE** . . . .

WINEMAKER (OR NAME OF PRODUCER) . . . .

Look, Smell & Taste

COLOR IS . . . .

SMELLS LIKE:

Fruity
- ○ Citrus
- ○ Tropical
- ○ Berry
- ○ Dried fruits

Veggie
- ○ Herby
- ○ Grassy
- ○ Green pepper
- ○ Minty

Bready
- ○ Yeasty

Floral
- ○ Orange blossom
- ○ Jasmine

Spicy
- ○ Pepper
- ○ Cloves
- ○ Cinnamon
- ○ Licorice

Woody
- ○ Smoky
- ○ Oaky
- ○ Vanilla

Earthy
- ○ Old socks
- ○ Musty
- ○ Moldy

Weird
- ○ Eggy
- ○ Burnt match
- ○ Cardboard

TASTES OF . . . .

. . . .

. . . .

Structure & Balance

THE ZIP (ACIDITY)
○ Low Buzz
○ Medium Bite
○ Lip-Tingling High

THE GRIP (TANNINS)
○ Big
○ Firm
○ Soft

THE OOMPH (BODY)
○ Light-bodied
○ Medium-bodied
○ Full-bodied

Three to five key words that will remind me what this wine was like ....

....

What I ate and how the wine matched ....

....

....

Takeaway tasting notes (look, smell, taste, and balance) ....

....

....

....

....

....

....

....

....

Date tasted . . . .

Okay   Pretty good   Will buy again

The Overview

WINE STYLE . . . .   **COUNTRY** . . . .

GRAPE(S) . . . .   **PRICE** . . . .

WINEMAKER (OR NAME OF PRODUCER) . . . .

Look, Smell & Taste

COLOR IS . . . .

SMELLS LIKE:

Fruity
- ○ Citrus
- ○ Tropical
- ○ Berry
- ○ Dried fruits

Veggie
- ○ Herby
- ○ Grassy
- ○ Green pepper
- ○ Minty

Bready
- ○ Yeasty

Floral
- ○ Orange blossom
- ○ Jasmine

Spicy
- ○ Pepper
- ○ Cloves
- ○ Cinnamon
- ○ Licorice

Woody
- ○ Smoky
- ○ Oaky
- ○ Vanilla

Earthy
- ○ Old socks
- ○ Musty
- ○ Moldy

Weird
- ○ Eggy
- ○ Burnt match
- ○ Cardboard

TASTES OF . . . .

. . . .

. . . .

Structure & Balance

THE ZIP (ACIDITY)
- Low Buzz
- Medium Bite
- Lip-Tingling High

THE GRIP (TANNINS)
- Big
- Firm
- Soft

THE OOMPH (BODY)
- Light-bodied
- Medium-bodied
- Full-bodied

Three to five key words that will remind me what this wine was like

What I ate and how the wine matched

Takeaway tasting notes (look, smell, taste, and balance)

Date tasted . . . .

Okay　　Pretty good　　Will buy again

The Overview

WINE STYLE . . . . **COUNTRY** . . . .

GRAPE(S) . . . . **PRICE** . . . .

WINEMAKER (OR NAME OF PRODUCER) . . . .

Look, Smell & Taste

COLOR IS . . . .

SMELLS LIKE:

Fruity
○ Citrus
○ Tropical
○ Berry
○ Dried fruits

Veggie
○ Herby
○ Grassy
○ Green pepper
○ Minty

Bready
○ Yeasty

Floral
○ Orange blossom
○ Jasmine

Spicy
○ Pepper
○ Cloves
○ Cinnamon
○ Licorice

Woody
○ Smoky
○ Oaky
○ Vanilla

Earthy
○ Old socks
○ Musty
○ Moldy

Weird
○ Eggy
○ Burnt match
○ Cardboard

TASTES OF . . . .

. . . .

. . . .

Structure & Balance

THE ZIP (ACIDITY)
- Low Buzz
- Medium Bite
- Lip-Tingling High

THE GRIP (TANNINS)
- Big
- Firm
- Soft

THE OOMPH (BODY)
- Light-bodied
- Medium-bodied
- Full-bodied

Three to five key words that will remind me what this wine was like

What I ate and how the wine matched

Takeaway tasting notes (look, smell, taste, and balance)

Date tasted . . . .

Okay   Pretty good   Will buy again

The Overview

WINE STYLE . . . .   **COUNTRY** . . . .

GRAPE(S) . . . .   **PRICE** . . . .

WINEMAKER (OR NAME OF PRODUCER) . . . .

Look, Smell & Taste

COLOR IS . . . .

SMELLS LIKE:

Fruity
- ○ Citrus
- ○ Tropical
- ○ Berry
- ○ Dried fruits

Veggie
- ○ Herby
- ○ Grassy
- ○ Green pepper
- ○ Minty

Bready
- ○ Yeasty

Floral
- ○ Orange blossom
- ○ Jasmine

Spicy
- ○ Pepper
- ○ Cloves
- ○ Cinnamon
- ○ Licorice

Woody
- ○ Smoky
- ○ Oaky
- ○ Vanilla

Earthy
- ○ Old socks
- ○ Musty
- ○ Moldy

Weird
- ○ Eggy
- ○ Burnt match
- ○ Cardboard

TASTES OF . . . .

. . . .

. . . .

Structure & Balance

THE ZIP (ACIDITY)
- ○ Low Buzz
- ○ Medium Bite
- ○ Lip-Tingling High

THE GRIP (TANNINS)
- ○ Big
- ○ Firm
- ○ Soft

THE OOMPH (BODY)
- ○ Light-bodied
- ○ Medium-bodied
- ○ Full-bodied

Three to five key words that will remind me what this wine was like ....

....

What I ate and how the wine matched ....

....

....

Takeaway tasting notes (look, smell, taste, and balance) ....

....

....

....

....

....

....

....

....

....

Date tasted ....

Okay   Pretty good   Will buy again

The Overview

WINE STYLE .... **COUNTRY** ....

GRAPE(S) .... **PRICE** ....

WINEMAKER (OR NAME OF PRODUCER) ....

Look, Smell & Taste

COLOR IS ....

SMELLS LIKE:

Fruity
- Citrus
- Tropical
- Berry
- Dried fruits

Veggie
- Herby
- Grassy
- Green pepper
- Minty

Bready
- Yeasty

Floral
- Orange blossom
- Jasmine

Spicy
- Pepper
- Cloves
- Cinnamon
- Licorice

Woody
- Smoky
- Oaky
- Vanilla

Earthy
- Old socks
- Musty
- Moldy

Weird
- Eggy
- Burnt match
- Cardboard

TASTES OF ....

....

....

Structure & Balance

THE ZIP (ACIDITY)
- Low Buzz
- Medium Bite
- Lip-Tingling High

THE GRIP (TANNINS)
- Big
- Firm
- Soft

THE OOMPH (BODY)
- Light-bodied
- Medium-bodied
- Full-bodied

Three to five key words that will remind me what this wine was like ....

....

What I ate and how the wine matched ....

....

....

Takeaway tasting notes (look, smell, taste, and balance) ....

....

....

....

....

....

....

....

....

....

Date tasted ....

Okay   Pretty good   Will buy again

The Overview

WINE STYLE ....   **COUNTRY** ....

GRAPE(S) ....   **PRICE** ....

WINEMAKER (OR NAME OF PRODUCER) ....

Look, Smell & Taste

COLOR IS ....

SMELLS LIKE:

Fruity
○ Citrus
○ Tropical
○ Berry
○ Dried fruits

Veggie
○ Herby
○ Grassy
○ Green pepper
○ Minty

Bready
○ Yeasty

Floral
○ Orange blossom
○ Jasmine

Spicy
○ Pepper
○ Cloves
○ Cinnamon
○ Licorice

Woody
○ Smoky
○ Oaky
○ Vanilla

Earthy
○ Old socks
○ Musty
○ Moldy

Weird
○ Eggy
○ Burnt match
○ Cardboard

TASTES OF ....

....

....

Structure & Balance

THE ZIP (ACIDITY)
- Low Buzz
- Medium Bite
- Lip-Tingling High

THE GRIP (TANNINS)
- Big
- Firm
- Soft

THE OOMPH (BODY)
- Light-bodied
- Medium-bodied
- Full-bodied

Three to five key words that will remind me what this wine was like ....
....

What I ate and how the wine matched ....
....
....

Takeaway tasting notes (look, smell, taste, and balance) ....
....
....
....
....
....
....
....
....
....

Date tasted . . . .

Okay   Pretty good   Will buy again

The Overview

WINE STYLE . . . . **COUNTRY** . . . .

GRAPE(S) . . . . **PRICE** . . . .

WINEMAKER (OR NAME OF PRODUCER) . . . .

Look, Smell & Taste

COLOR IS . . . .

SMELLS LIKE:

Fruity
○ Citrus
○ Tropical
○ Berry
○ Dried fruits

Veggie
○ Herby
○ Grassy
○ Green pepper
○ Minty

Bready
○ Yeasty

Floral
○ Orange blossom
○ Jasmine

Spicy
○ Pepper
○ Cloves
○ Cinnamon
○ Licorice

Woody
○ Smoky
○ Oaky
○ Vanilla

Earthy
○ Old socks
○ Musty
○ Moldy

Weird
○ Eggy
○ Burnt match
○ Cardboard

TASTES OF . . . .

. . . .

. . . .

Structure & Balance

THE ZIP (ACIDITY)
- ○ Low Buzz
- ○ Medium Bite
- ○ Lip-Tingling High

THE GRIP (TANNINS)
- ○ Big
- ○ Firm
- ○ Soft

THE OOMPH (BODY)
- ○ Light-bodied
- ○ Medium-bodied
- ○ Full-bodied

Three to five key words that will remind me what this wine was like

What I ate and how the wine matched

Takeaway tasting notes (look, smell, taste, and balance)

Date tasted . . . .

Okay   Pretty good   Will buy again

The Overview

WINE STYLE . . . .   **COUNTRY** . . . .

GRAPE(S) . . . .   **PRICE** . . . .

WINEMAKER (OR NAME OF PRODUCER) . . . .

Look, Smell & Taste

COLOR IS . . . .

SMELLS LIKE:

Fruity
○ Citrus
○ Tropical
○ Berry
○ Dried fruits

Veggie
○ Herby
○ Grassy
○ Green pepper
○ Minty

Bready
○ Yeasty

Floral
○ Orange blossom
○ Jasmine

Spicy
○ Pepper
○ Cloves
○ Cinnamon
○ Licorice

Woody
○ Smoky
○ Oaky
○ Vanilla

Earthy
○ Old socks
○ Musty
○ Moldy

Weird
○ Eggy
○ Burnt match
○ Cardboard

TASTES OF . . . .

. . . .

. . . .

Structure & Balance

THE ZIP (ACIDITY)
○ Low Buzz
○ Medium Bite
○ Lip-Tingling High

THE GRIP (TANNINS)
○ Big
○ Firm
○ Soft

THE OOMPH (BODY)
○ Light-bodied
○ Medium-bodied
○ Full-bodied

Three to five key words that will remind me what this wine was like

What I ate and how the wine matched

Takeaway tasting notes (look, smell, taste, and balance)

Okay   Pretty good   Will buy again

The Overview

WINE STYLE . . . .   **COUNTRY** . . . .

GRAPE(S) . . . .   **PRICE** . . . .

WINEMAKER (OR NAME OF PRODUCER) . . . .

Look, Smell & Taste

COLOR IS . . . .

SMELLS LIKE:

Fruity
- ○ Citrus
- ○ Tropical
- ○ Berry
- ○ Dried fruits

Veggie
- ○ Herby
- ○ Grassy
- ○ Green pepper
- ○ Minty

Bready
- ○ Yeasty

Floral
- ○ Orange blossom
- ○ Jasmine

Spicy
- ○ Pepper
- ○ Cloves
- ○ Cinnamon
- ○ Licorice

Woody
- ○ Smoky
- ○ Oaky
- ○ Vanilla

Earthy
- ○ Old socks
- ○ Musty
- ○ Moldy

Weird
- ○ Eggy
- ○ Burnt match
- ○ Cardboard

TASTES OF . . . .

. . . .

. . . .

Structure & Balance

THE ZIP (ACIDITY)
- ○ Low Buzz
- ○ Medium Bite
- ○ Lip-Tingling High

THE GRIP (TANNINS)
- ○ Big
- ○ Firm
- ○ Soft

THE OOMPH (BODY)
- ○ Light-bodied
- ○ Medium-bodied
- ○ Full-bodied

Three to five key words that will remind me what this wine was like ....
....

What I ate and how the wine matched ....
....
....

Takeaway tasting notes (look, smell, taste, and balance) ....
....
....
....
....
....
....
....
....
....

Date tasted ....

Okay   Pretty good   Will buy again

The Overview

WINE STYLE ....   **COUNTRY** ....

GRAPE(S) ....   **PRICE** ....

WINEMAKER (OR NAME OF PRODUCER) ....

Look, Smell & Taste

COLOR IS ....

SMELLS LIKE:

Fruity
○ Citrus
○ Tropical
○ Berry
○ Dried fruits

Veggie
○ Herby
○ Grassy
○ Green pepper
○ Minty

Bready
○ Yeasty

Floral
○ Orange blossom
○ Jasmine

Spicy
○ Pepper
○ Cloves
○ Cinnamon
○ Licorice

Woody
○ Smoky
○ Oaky
○ Vanilla

Earthy
○ Old socks
○ Musty
○ Moldy

Weird
○ Eggy
○ Burnt match
○ Cardboard

TASTES OF ....

....

....

Structure & Balance

THE ZIP (ACIDITY)
- Low Buzz
- Medium Bite
- Lip-Tingling High

THE GRIP (TANNINS)
- Big
- Firm
- Soft

THE OOMPH (BODY)
- Light-bodied
- Medium-bodied
- Full-bodied

Three to five key words that will remind me what this wine was like

What I ate and how the wine matched

Takeaway tasting notes (look, smell, taste, and balance)

Date tasted . . . .

Okay   Pretty good   Will buy again

The Overview

WINE STYLE . . . . **COUNTRY** . . . .

GRAPE(S) . . . . **PRICE** . . . .

WINEMAKER (OR NAME OF PRODUCER) . . . .

Look, Smell & Taste

COLOR IS . . . .

SMELLS LIKE:

Fruity
- Citrus
- Tropical
- Berry
- Dried fruits

Veggie
- Herby
- Grassy
- Green pepper
- Minty

Bready
- Yeasty

Floral
- Orange blossom
- Jasmine

Spicy
- Pepper
- Cloves
- Cinnamon
- Licorice

Woody
- Smoky
- Oaky
- Vanilla

Earthy
- Old socks
- Musty
- Moldy

Weird
- Eggy
- Burnt match
- Cardboard

TASTES OF . . . .

. . . .

. . . .

Structure & Balance

THE ZIP (ACIDITY)
- ○ Low Buzz
- ○ Medium Bite
- ○ Lip-Tingling High

THE GRIP (TANNINS)
- ○ Big
- ○ Firm
- ○ Soft

THE OOMPH (BODY)
- ○ Light-bodied
- ○ Medium-bodied
- ○ Full-bodied

Three to five key words that will remind me what this wine was like ....

....

What I ate and how the wine matched ....

....

....

Takeaway tasting notes (look, smell, taste, and balance) ....

....

....

....

....

....

....

....

....

....

Date tasted ....

Okay   Pretty good   Will buy again

The Overview

WINE STYLE ....   **COUNTRY** ....

GRAPE(S) ....   **PRICE** ....

WINEMAKER (OR NAME OF PRODUCER) ....

Look, Smell & Taste

COLOR IS ....

SMELLS LIKE:

Fruity
- ○ Citrus
- ○ Tropical
- ○ Berry
- ○ Dried fruits

Veggie
- ○ Herby
- ○ Grassy
- ○ Green pepper
- ○ Minty

Bready
- ○ Yeasty

Floral
- ○ Orange blossom
- ○ Jasmine

Spicy
- ○ Pepper
- ○ Cloves
- ○ Cinnamon
- ○ Licorice

Woody
- ○ Smoky
- ○ Oaky
- ○ Vanilla

Earthy
- ○ Old socks
- ○ Musty
- ○ Moldy

Weird
- ○ Eggy
- ○ Burnt match
- ○ Cardboard

TASTES OF ....

....

....

Structure & Balance

THE ZIP (ACIDITY)
- ○ Low Buzz
- ○ Medium Bite
- ○ Lip-Tingling High

THE GRIP (TANNINS)
- ○ Big
- ○ Firm
- ○ Soft

THE OOMPH (BODY)
- ○ Light-bodied
- ○ Medium-bodied
- ○ Full-bodied

Three to five key words that will remind me what this wine was like ....

....

What I ate and how the wine matched ....

....

....

Takeaway tasting notes (look, smell, taste, and balance) ....

....

....

....

....

....

....

....

....

Date tasted ....

Okay   Pretty good   Will buy again

The Overview

WINE STYLE ....   **COUNTRY** ....

GRAPE(S) ....   **PRICE** ....

WINEMAKER (OR NAME OF PRODUCER) ....

Look, Smell & Taste

COLOR IS ....

SMELLS LIKE:

Fruity
- ○ Citrus
- ○ Tropical
- ○ Berry
- ○ Dried fruits

Veggie
- ○ Herby
- ○ Grassy
- ○ Green pepper
- ○ Minty

Bready
- ○ Yeasty

Floral
- ○ Orange blossom
- ○ Jasmine

Spicy
- ○ Pepper
- ○ Cloves
- ○ Cinnamon
- ○ Licorice

Woody
- ○ Smoky
- ○ Oaky
- ○ Vanilla

Earthy
- ○ Old socks
- ○ Musty
- ○ Moldy

Weird
- ○ Eggy
- ○ Burnt match
- ○ Cardboard

TASTES OF ....

....

....

Structure & Balance

THE ZIP (ACIDITY)
- ○ Low Buzz
- ○ Medium Bite
- ○ Lip-Tingling High

THE GRIP (TANNINS)
- ○ Big
- ○ Firm
- ○ Soft

THE OOMPH (BODY)
- ○ Light-bodied
- ○ Medium-bodied
- ○ Full-bodied

Three to five key words that will remind me what this wine was like ....

....

What I ate and how the wine matched ....

....

....

Takeaway tasting notes (look, smell, taste, and balance) ....

....

....

....

....

....

....

....

....

....

Date tasted . . . .

Okay   Pretty good   Will buy again

The Overview

WINE STYLE . . . . **COUNTRY** . . . .

GRAPE(S) . . . . **PRICE** . . . .

WINEMAKER (OR NAME OF PRODUCER) . . . .

Look, Smell & Taste

COLOR IS . . . .

SMELLS LIKE:

Fruity
- Citrus
- Tropical
- Berry
- Dried fruits

Veggie
- Herby
- Grassy
- Green pepper
- Minty

Bready
- Yeasty

Floral
- Orange blossom
- Jasmine

Spicy
- Pepper
- Cloves
- Cinnamon
- Licorice

Woody
- Smoky
- Oaky
- Vanilla

Earthy
- Old socks
- Musty
- Moldy

Weird
- Eggy
- Burnt match
- Cardboard

TASTES OF . . . .

. . . .

. . . .

Structure & Balance

THE ZIP (ACIDITY)
- ○ Low Buzz
- ○ Medium Bite
- ○ Lip-Tingling High

THE GRIP (TANNINS)
- ○ Big
- ○ Firm
- ○ Soft

THE OOMPH (BODY)
- ○ Light-bodied
- ○ Medium-bodied
- ○ Full-bodied

Three to five key words that will remind me what this wine was like ....

....

What I ate and how the wine matched ....

....

....

Takeaway tasting notes (look, smell, taste, and balance) ....

....

....

....

....

....

....

....

....

Date tasted . . . .

Okay   Pretty good   Will buy again

The Overview

WINE STYLE . . . .   **COUNTRY** . . . .

GRAPE(S) . . . .   **PRICE** . . . .

WINEMAKER (OR NAME OF PRODUCER) . . . .

Look, Smell & Taste

COLOR IS . . . .

SMELLS LIKE:

Fruity
○ Citrus
○ Tropical
○ Berry
○ Dried fruits

Veggie
○ Herby
○ Grassy
○ Green pepper
○ Minty

Bready
○ Yeasty

Floral
○ Orange blossom
○ Jasmine

Spicy
○ Pepper
○ Cloves
○ Cinnamon
○ Licorice

Woody
○ Smoky
○ Oaky
○ Vanilla

Earthy
○ Old socks
○ Musty
○ Moldy

Weird
○ Eggy
○ Burnt match
○ Cardboard

TASTES OF . . . .

. . . .

. . . .

Structure & Balance

THE ZIP (ACIDITY)
- Low Buzz
- Medium Bite
- Lip-Tingling High

THE GRIP (TANNINS)
- Big
- Firm
- Soft

THE OOMPH (BODY)
- Light-bodied
- Medium-bodied
- Full-bodied

Three to five key words that will remind me what this wine was like . . . .

What I ate and how the wine matched . . . .

Takeaway tasting notes (look, smell, taste, and balance) . . . .

Date tasted . . . .

☆ ☆ ☆ ☆ ☆
Okay   Pretty good   Will buy again

The Overview

WINE STYLE . . . . **COUNTRY** . . . .

GRAPE(S) . . . . **PRICE** . . . .

WINEMAKER (OR NAME OF PRODUCER) . . . .

Look, Smell & Taste

COLOR IS . . . .

SMELLS LIKE:

Fruity
○ Citrus
○ Tropical
○ Berry
○ Dried fruits

Veggie
○ Herby
○ Grassy
○ Green pepper
○ Minty

Bready
○ Yeasty

Floral
○ Orange blossom
○ Jasmine

Spicy
○ Pepper
○ Cloves
○ Cinnamon
○ Licorice

Woody
○ Smoky
○ Oaky
○ Vanilla

Earthy
○ Old socks
○ Musty
○ Moldy

Weird
○ Eggy
○ Burnt match
○ Cardboard

TASTES OF . . . .

. . . .

. . . .

Structure & Balance

THE ZIP (ACIDITY)
- ○ Low Buzz
- ○ Medium Bite
- ○ Lip-Tingling High

THE GRIP (TANNINS)
- ○ Big
- ○ Firm
- ○ Soft

THE OOMPH (BODY)
- ○ Light-bodied
- ○ Medium-bodied
- ○ Full-bodied

Three to five key words that will remind me what this wine was like . . . .

. . . .

What I ate and how the wine matched . . . .

. . . .

. . . .

Takeaway tasting notes (look, smell, taste, and balance) . . . .

. . . .

. . . .

. . . .

. . . .

. . . .

. . . .

. . . .

. . . .

Date tasted ....

Okay   Pretty good   Will buy again

The Overview

WINE STYLE ....   **COUNTRY** ....

GRAPE(S) ....   **PRICE** ....

WINEMAKER (OR NAME OF PRODUCER) ....

Look, Smell & Taste

COLOR IS ....

SMELLS LIKE:

Fruity
- Citrus
- Tropical
- Berry
- Dried fruits

Veggie
- Herby
- Grassy
- Green pepper
- Minty

Bready
- Yeasty

Floral
- Orange blossom
- Jasmine

Spicy
- Pepper
- Cloves
- Cinnamon
- Licorice

Woody
- Smoky
- Oaky
- Vanilla

Earthy
- Old socks
- Musty
- Moldy

Weird
- Eggy
- Burnt match
- Cardboard

TASTES OF ....

....

....

Structure & Balance

THE ZIP (ACIDITY)
- Low Buzz
- Medium Bite
- Lip-Tingling High

THE GRIP (TANNINS)
- Big
- Firm
- Soft

THE OOMPH (BODY)
- Light-bodied
- Medium-bodied
- Full-bodied

Three to five key words that will remind me what this wine was like

What I ate and how the wine matched

Takeaway tasting notes (look, smell, taste, and balance)

Date tasted ....

Okay   Pretty good   Will buy again

The Overview

WINE STYLE .... **COUNTRY** ....

GRAPE(S) .... **PRICE** ....

WINEMAKER (OR NAME OF PRODUCER) ....

Look, Smell & Taste

COLOR IS ....

SMELLS LIKE:

Fruity
○ Citrus
○ Tropical
○ Berry
○ Dried fruits

Veggie
○ Herby
○ Grassy
○ Green pepper
○ Minty

Bready
○ Yeasty

Floral
○ Orange blossom
○ Jasmine

Spicy
○ Pepper
○ Cloves
○ Cinnamon
○ Licorice

Woody
○ Smoky
○ Oaky
○ Vanilla

Earthy
○ Old socks
○ Musty
○ Moldy

Weird
○ Eggy
○ Burnt match
○ Cardboard

TASTES OF ....

....

....

Structure & Balance

THE ZIP (ACIDITY)
- Low Buzz
- Medium Bite
- Lip-Tingling High

THE GRIP (TANNINS)
- Big
- Firm
- Soft

THE OOMPH (BODY)
- Light-bodied
- Medium-bodied
- Full-bodied

Three to five key words that will remind me what this wine was like ....

....

What I ate and how the wine matched ....

....

....

Takeaway tasting notes (look, smell, taste, and balance) ....

....

....

....

....

....

....

....

....

....

Date tasted ....

Okay   Pretty good   Will buy again

The Overview

WINE STYLE ....   **COUNTRY** ....

GRAPE(S) ....   **PRICE** ....

WINEMAKER (OR NAME OF PRODUCER) ....

Look, Smell & Taste

COLOR IS ....

SMELLS LIKE:

Fruity
- Citrus
- Tropical
- Berry
- Dried fruits

Veggie
- Herby
- Grassy
- Green pepper
- Minty

Bready
- Yeasty

Floral
- Orange blossom
- Jasmine

Spicy
- Pepper
- Cloves
- Cinnamon
- Licorice

Woody
- Smoky
- Oaky
- Vanilla

Earthy
- Old socks
- Musty
- Moldy

Weird
- Eggy
- Burnt match
- Cardboard

TASTES OF ....

....

....

Structure & Balance

THE ZIP (ACIDITY)
- ○ Low Buzz
- ○ Medium Bite
- ○ Lip-Tingling High

THE GRIP (TANNINS)
- ○ Big
- ○ Firm
- ○ Soft

THE OOMPH (BODY)
- ○ Light-bodied
- ○ Medium-bodied
- ○ Full-bodied

Three to five key words that will remind me what this wine was like . . . .

What I ate and how the wine matched . . . .

Takeaway tasting notes (look, smell, taste, and balance) . . . .

Date tasted . . . .

Okay   Pretty good   Will buy again

The Overview

WINE STYLE . . . .   **COUNTRY** . . . .

GRAPE(S) . . . .   **PRICE** . . . .

WINEMAKER (OR NAME OF PRODUCER) . . . .

Look, Smell & Taste

COLOR IS . . . .

SMELLS LIKE:

Fruity
○ Citrus
○ Tropical
○ Berry
○ Dried fruits

Veggie
○ Herby
○ Grassy
○ Green pepper
○ Minty

Bready
○ Yeasty

Floral
○ Orange blossom
○ Jasmine

Spicy
○ Pepper
○ Cloves
○ Cinnamon
○ Licorice

Woody
○ Smoky
○ Oaky
○ Vanilla

Earthy
○ Old socks
○ Musty
○ Moldy

Weird
○ Eggy
○ Burnt match
○ Cardboard

TASTES OF . . . .

. . . .

. . . .

Structure & Balance

THE ZIP (ACIDITY)
○ Low Buzz
○ Medium Bite
○ Lip-Tingling High

THE GRIP (TANNINS)
○ Big
○ Firm
○ Soft

THE OOMPH (BODY)
○ Light-bodied
○ Medium-bodied
○ Full-bodied

Three to five key words that will remind me what this wine was like

What I ate and how the wine matched

Takeaway tasting notes (look, smell, taste, and balance)

Date tasted ....

Okay   Pretty good   Will buy again

The Overview

WINE STYLE .... **COUNTRY** ....

GRAPE(S) .... **PRICE** ....

WINEMAKER (OR NAME OF PRODUCER) ....

Look, Smell & Taste

COLOR IS ....

SMELLS LIKE:

Fruity
○ Citrus
○ Tropical
○ Berry
○ Dried fruits

Veggie
○ Herby
○ Grassy
○ Green pepper
○ Minty

Bready
○ Yeasty

Floral
○ Orange blossom
○ Jasmine

Spicy
○ Pepper
○ Cloves
○ Cinnamon
○ Licorice

Woody
○ Smoky
○ Oaky
○ Vanilla

Earthy
○ Old socks
○ Musty
○ Moldy

Weird
○ Eggy
○ Burnt match
○ Cardboard

TASTES OF ....

....

....

Structure & Balance

THE ZIP (ACIDITY)
- Low Buzz
- Medium Bite
- Lip-Tingling High

THE GRIP (TANNINS)
- Big
- Firm
- Soft

THE OOMPH (BODY)
- Light-bodied
- Medium-bodied
- Full-bodied

Three to five key words that will remind me what this wine was like ....

....

What I ate and how the wine matched ....

....

....

Takeaway tasting notes (look, smell, taste, and balance) ....

....

....

....

....

....

....

....

....

....

Date tasted . . . .

Okay   Pretty good   Will buy again

The Overview

WINE STYLE . . . . **COUNTRY** . . . .

GRAPE(S) . . . . **PRICE** . . . .

WINEMAKER (OR NAME OF PRODUCER) . . . .

Look, Smell & Taste

COLOR IS . . . .

SMELLS LIKE:

Fruity
- ○ Citrus
- ○ Tropical
- ○ Berry
- ○ Dried fruits

Veggie
- ○ Herby
- ○ Grassy
- ○ Green pepper
- ○ Minty

Bready
- ○ Yeasty

Floral
- ○ Orange blossom
- ○ Jasmine

Spicy
- ○ Pepper
- ○ Cloves
- ○ Cinnamon
- ○ Licorice

Woody
- ○ Smoky
- ○ Oaky
- ○ Vanilla

Earthy
- ○ Old socks
- ○ Musty
- ○ Moldy

Weird
- ○ Eggy
- ○ Burnt match
- ○ Cardboard

TASTES OF . . . .

. . . .

. . . .

Structure & Balance

THE ZIP (ACIDITY)
○ Low Buzz
○ Medium Bite
○ Lip-Tingling High

THE GRIP (TANNINS)
○ Big
○ Firm
○ Soft

THE OOMPH (BODY)
○ Light-bodied
○ Medium-bodied
○ Full-bodied

Three to five key words that will remind me what this wine was like

What I ate and how the wine matched

Takeaway tasting notes (look, smell, taste, and balance)

Date tasted . . . .

Okay   Pretty good   Will buy again

The Overview

WINE STYLE . . . . **COUNTRY** . . . .

GRAPE(S) . . . . **PRICE** . . . .

WINEMAKER (OR NAME OF PRODUCER) . . . .

Look, Smell & Taste

COLOR IS . . . .

SMELLS LIKE:

Fruity
- Citrus
- Tropical
- Berry
- Dried fruits

Veggie
- Herby
- Grassy
- Green pepper
- Minty

Bready
- Yeasty

Floral
- Orange blossom
- Jasmine

Spicy
- Pepper
- Cloves
- Cinnamon
- Licorice

Woody
- Smoky
- Oaky
- Vanilla

Earthy
- Old socks
- Musty
- Moldy

Weird
- Eggy
- Burnt match
- Cardboard

TASTES OF . . . .

. . . .

. . . .

Structure & Balance

THE ZIP (ACIDITY)
- Low Buzz
- Medium Bite
- Lip-Tingling High

THE GRIP (TANNINS)
- Big
- Firm
- Soft

THE OOMPH (BODY)
- Light-bodied
- Medium-bodied
- Full-bodied

Three to five key words that will remind me what this wine was like

What I ate and how the wine matched

Takeaway tasting notes (look, smell, taste, and balance)

Okay   Pretty good   Will buy again

The Overview

WINE STYLE .... **COUNTRY** ....

GRAPE(S) .... **PRICE** ....

WINEMAKER (OR NAME OF PRODUCER) ....

Look, Smell & Taste

COLOR IS ....

SMELLS LIKE:

Fruity
○ Citrus
○ Tropical
○ Berry
○ Dried fruits

Veggie
○ Herby
○ Grassy
○ Green pepper
○ Minty

Bready
○ Yeasty

Floral
○ Orange blossom
○ Jasmine

Spicy
○ Pepper
○ Cloves
○ Cinnamon
○ Licorice

Woody
○ Smoky
○ Oaky
○ Vanilla

Earthy
○ Old socks
○ Musty
○ Moldy

Weird
○ Eggy
○ Burnt match
○ Cardboard

TASTES OF ....

....

....

Structure & Balance

THE ZIP (ACIDITY)
- Low Buzz
- Medium Bite
- Lip-Tingling High

THE GRIP (TANNINS)
- Big
- Firm
- Soft

THE OOMPH (BODY)
- Light-bodied
- Medium-bodied
- Full-bodied

Three to five key words that will remind me what this wine was like ....

....

What I ate and how the wine matched ....

....

....

Takeaway tasting notes (look, smell, taste, and balance) ....

....

....

....

....

....

....

....

....

....

Date tasted ....

Okay   Pretty good   Will buy again

The Overview

WINE STYLE .... **COUNTRY** ....

GRAPE(S) .... **PRICE** ....

WINEMAKER (OR NAME OF PRODUCER) ....

Look, Smell & Taste

COLOR IS ....

SMELLS LIKE:

Fruity
- Citrus
- Tropical
- Berry
- Dried fruits

Veggie
- Herby
- Grassy
- Green pepper
- Minty

Bready
- Yeasty

Floral
- Orange blossom
- Jasmine

Spicy
- Pepper
- Cloves
- Cinnamon
- Licorice

Woody
- Smoky
- Oaky
- Vanilla

Earthy
- Old socks
- Musty
- Moldy

Weird
- Eggy
- Burnt match
- Cardboard

TASTES OF ....

....

....

Structure & Balance

THE ZIP (ACIDITY)
○ Low Buzz
○ Medium Bite
○ Lip-Tingling High

THE GRIP (TANNINS)
○ Big
○ Firm
○ Soft

THE OOMPH (BODY)
○ Light-bodied
○ Medium-bodied
○ Full-bodied

Three to five key words that will remind me what this wine was like

What I ate and how the wine matched

Takeaway tasting notes (look, smell, taste, and balance)

Date tasted . . . .

Okay　　　　Pretty good　　Will buy again

The Overview

WINE STYLE . . . . **COUNTRY** . . . .

GRAPE(S) . . . . **PRICE** . . . .

WINEMAKER (OR NAME OF PRODUCER) . . . .

Look, Smell & Taste

COLOR IS . . . .

SMELLS LIKE:

Fruity
- ○ Citrus
- ○ Tropical
- ○ Berry
- ○ Dried fruits

Veggie
- ○ Herby
- ○ Grassy
- ○ Green pepper
- ○ Minty

Bready
- ○ Yeasty

Floral
- ○ Orange blossom
- ○ Jasmine

Spicy
- ○ Pepper
- ○ Cloves
- ○ Cinnamon
- ○ Licorice

Woody
- ○ Smoky
- ○ Oaky
- ○ Vanilla

Earthy
- ○ Old socks
- ○ Musty
- ○ Moldy

Weird
- ○ Eggy
- ○ Burnt match
- ○ Cardboard

TASTES OF . . . .

. . . .

. . . .

Structure & Balance

THE ZIP (ACIDITY)
- Low Buzz
- Medium Bite
- Lip-Tingling High

THE GRIP (TANNINS)
- Big
- Firm
- Soft

THE OOMPH (BODY)
- Light-bodied
- Medium-bodied
- Full-bodied

Three to five key words that will remind me what this wine was like ....

....

What I ate and how the wine matched ....

....

....

Takeaway tasting notes (look, smell, taste, and balance) ....

....

....

....

....

....

....

....

....

....

Date tasted . . . .

Okay   Pretty good   Will buy again

The Overview

WINE STYLE . . . . **COUNTRY** . . . .

GRAPE(S) . . . . **PRICE** . . . .

WINEMAKER (OR NAME OF PRODUCER) . . . .

Look, Smell & Taste

COLOR IS . . . .

SMELLS LIKE:

Fruity
- Citrus
- Tropical
- Berry
- Dried fruits

Veggie
- Herby
- Grassy
- Green pepper
- Minty

Bready
- Yeasty

Floral
- Orange blossom
- Jasmine

Spicy
- Pepper
- Cloves
- Cinnamon
- Licorice

Woody
- Smoky
- Oaky
- Vanilla

Earthy
- Old socks
- Musty
- Moldy

Weird
- Eggy
- Burnt match
- Cardboard

TASTES OF . . . .

. . . .

. . . .

Structure & Balance

THE ZIP (ACIDITY)
- Low Buzz
- Medium Bite
- Lip-Tingling High

THE GRIP (TANNINS)
- Big
- Firm
- Soft

THE OOMPH (BODY)
- Light-bodied
- Medium-bodied
- Full-bodied

Three to five key words that will remind me what this wine was like ....
....

What I ate and how the wine matched ....
....
....

Takeaway tasting notes (look, smell, taste, and balance) ....
....
....
....
....
....
....
....
....
....

Date tasted ....

Okay   Pretty good   Will buy again

The Overview

WINE STYLE .... **COUNTRY** ....

GRAPE(S) .... **PRICE** ....

WINEMAKER (OR NAME OF PRODUCER) ....

Look, Smell & Taste

COLOR IS ....

SMELLS LIKE:

Fruity
- ○ Citrus
- ○ Tropical
- ○ Berry
- ○ Dried fruits

Veggie
- ○ Herby
- ○ Grassy
- ○ Green pepper
- ○ Minty

Bready
- ○ Yeasty

Floral
- ○ Orange blossom
- ○ Jasmine

Spicy
- ○ Pepper
- ○ Cloves
- ○ Cinnamon
- ○ Licorice

Woody
- ○ Smoky
- ○ Oaky
- ○ Vanilla

Earthy
- ○ Old socks
- ○ Musty
- ○ Moldy

Weird
- ○ Eggy
- ○ Burnt match
- ○ Cardboard

TASTES OF ....

....

....

Structure & Balance

THE ZIP (ACIDITY)
- Low Buzz
- Medium Bite
- Lip-Tingling High

THE GRIP (TANNINS)
- Big
- Firm
- Soft

THE OOMPH (BODY)
- Light-bodied
- Medium-bodied
- Full-bodied

Three to five key words that will remind me what this wine was like ....

....

What I ate and how the wine matched ....

....

....

Takeaway tasting notes (look, smell, taste, and balance) ....

....

....

....

....

....

....

....

....

Date tasted ....

Okay   Pretty good   Will buy again

The Overview

WINE STYLE ....   **COUNTRY** ....

GRAPE(S) ....   **PRICE** ....

WINEMAKER (OR NAME OF PRODUCER) ....

Look, Smell & Taste

COLOR IS ....

SMELLS LIKE:

Fruity
- ○ Citrus
- ○ Tropical
- ○ Berry
- ○ Dried fruits

Veggie
- ○ Herby
- ○ Grassy
- ○ Green pepper
- ○ Minty

Bready
- ○ Yeasty

Floral
- ○ Orange blossom
- ○ Jasmine

Spicy
- ○ Pepper
- ○ Cloves
- ○ Cinnamon
- ○ Licorice

Woody
- ○ Smoky
- ○ Oaky
- ○ Vanilla

Earthy
- ○ Old socks
- ○ Musty
- ○ Moldy

Weird
- ○ Eggy
- ○ Burnt match
- ○ Cardboard

TASTES OF ....

....

....

Structure & Balance

THE ZIP (ACIDITY)
- ○ Low Buzz
- ○ Medium Bite
- ○ Lip-Tingling High

THE GRIP (TANNINS)
- ○ Big
- ○ Firm
- ○ Soft

THE OOMPH (BODY)
- ○ Light-bodied
- ○ Medium-bodied
- ○ Full-bodied

Three to five key words that will remind me what this wine was like ....

....

What I ate and how the wine matched ....

....

....

Takeaway tasting notes (look, smell, taste, and balance) ....

....

....

....

....

....

....

....

....

....

Date tasted . . . .

Okay   Pretty good   Will buy again

The Overview

WINE STYLE . . . .   **COUNTRY** . . . .

GRAPE(S) . . . .   **PRICE** . . . .

WINEMAKER (OR NAME OF PRODUCER) . . . .

Look, Smell & Taste

COLOR IS . . . .

SMELLS LIKE:

Fruity
- ○ Citrus
- ○ Tropical
- ○ Berry
- ○ Dried fruits

Veggie
- ○ Herby
- ○ Grassy
- ○ Green pepper
- ○ Minty

Bready
- ○ Yeasty

Floral
- ○ Orange blossom
- ○ Jasmine

Spicy
- ○ Pepper
- ○ Cloves
- ○ Cinnamon
- ○ Licorice

Woody
- ○ Smoky
- ○ Oaky
- ○ Vanilla

Earthy
- ○ Old socks
- ○ Musty
- ○ Moldy

Weird
- ○ Eggy
- ○ Burnt match
- ○ Cardboard

TASTES OF . . . .

. . . .

. . . .

Structure & Balance

THE ZIP (ACIDITY)
- Low Buzz
- Medium Bite
- Lip-Tingling High

THE GRIP (TANNINS)
- Big
- Firm
- Soft

THE OOMPH (BODY)
- Light-bodied
- Medium-bodied
- Full-bodied

Three to five key words that will remind me what this wine was like ....

What I ate and how the wine matched ....

Takeaway tasting notes (look, smell, taste, and balance) ....

Date tasted . . . .

Okay   Pretty good   Will buy again

The Overview

WINE STYLE . . . . **COUNTRY** . . . .

GRAPE(S) . . . . **PRICE** . . . .

WINEMAKER (OR NAME OF PRODUCER) . . . .

Look, Smell & Taste

COLOR IS . . . .

SMELLS LIKE:

Fruity
- ○ Citrus
- ○ Tropical
- ○ Berry
- ○ Dried fruits

Veggie
- ○ Herby
- ○ Grassy
- ○ Green pepper
- ○ Minty

Bready
- ○ Yeasty

Floral
- ○ Orange blossom
- ○ Jasmine

Spicy
- ○ Pepper
- ○ Cloves
- ○ Cinnamon
- ○ Licorice

Woody
- ○ Smoky
- ○ Oaky
- ○ Vanilla

Earthy
- ○ Old socks
- ○ Musty
- ○ Moldy

Weird
- ○ Eggy
- ○ Burnt match
- ○ Cardboard

TASTES OF . . . .

. . . .

. . . .

Structure & Balance

THE ZIP (ACIDITY)
- ○ Low Buzz
- ○ Medium Bite
- ○ Lip-Tingling High

THE GRIP (TANNINS)
- ○ Big
- ○ Firm
- ○ Soft

THE OOMPH (BODY)
- ○ Light-bodied
- ○ Medium-bodied
- ○ Full-bodied

Three to five key words that will remind me what this wine was like ....

....

What I ate and how the wine matched ....

....

....

Takeaway tasting notes (look, smell, taste, and balance) ....

....

....

....

....

....

....

....

....

Date tasted . . . .

Okay   Pretty good   Will buy again

The Overview

WINE STYLE . . . .   **COUNTRY** . . . .

GRAPE(S) . . . .   **PRICE** . . . .

WINEMAKER (OR NAME OF PRODUCER) . . . .

Look, Smell & Taste

COLOR IS . . . .

SMELLS LIKE:

Fruity
○ Citrus
○ Tropical
○ Berry
○ Dried fruits

Veggie
○ Herby
○ Grassy
○ Green pepper
○ Minty

Bready
○ Yeasty

Floral
○ Orange blossom
○ Jasmine

Spicy
○ Pepper
○ Cloves
○ Cinnamon
○ Licorice

Woody
○ Smoky
○ Oaky
○ Vanilla

Earthy
○ Old socks
○ Musty
○ Moldy

Weird
○ Eggy
○ Burnt match
○ Cardboard

TASTES OF . . . .

. . . .

. . . .

Structure & Balance

THE ZIP (ACIDITY)
- Low Buzz
- Medium Bite
- Lip-Tingling High

THE GRIP (TANNINS)
- Big
- Firm
- Soft

THE OOMPH (BODY)
- Light-bodied
- Medium-bodied
- Full-bodied

Three to five key words that will remind me what this wine was like

What I ate and how the wine matched

Takeaway tasting notes (look, smell, taste, and balance)

Date tasted ....

Okay　　Pretty good　　Will buy again

The Overview

WINE STYLE .... **COUNTRY** ....

GRAPE(S) .... **PRICE** ....

WINEMAKER (OR NAME OF PRODUCER) ....

Look, Smell & Taste

COLOR IS ....

SMELLS LIKE:

Fruity
- Citrus
- Tropical
- Berry
- Dried fruits

Veggie
- Herby
- Grassy
- Green pepper
- Minty

Bready
- Yeasty

Floral
- Orange blossom
- Jasmine

Spicy
- Pepper
- Cloves
- Cinnamon
- Licorice

Woody
- Smoky
- Oaky
- Vanilla

Earthy
- Old socks
- Musty
- Moldy

Weird
- Eggy
- Burnt match
- Cardboard

TASTES OF ....
....
....

Structure & Balance

THE ZIP (ACIDITY)
- Low Buzz
- Medium Bite
- Lip-Tingling High

THE GRIP (TANNINS)
- Big
- Firm
- Soft

THE OOMPH (BODY)
- Light-bodied
- Medium-bodied
- Full-bodied

Three to five key words that will remind me what this wine was like

What I ate and how the wine matched

Takeaway tasting notes (look, smell, taste, and balance)

Date tasted ....

Okay   Pretty good   Will buy again

The Overview

WINE STYLE .... **COUNTRY** ....

GRAPE(S) .... **PRICE** ....

WINEMAKER (OR NAME OF PRODUCER) ....

Look, Smell & Taste

COLOR IS ....

SMELLS LIKE:

Fruity
- Citrus
- Tropical
- Berry
- Dried fruits

Veggie
- Herby
- Grassy
- Green pepper
- Minty

Bready
- Yeasty

Floral
- Orange blossom
- Jasmine

Spicy
- Pepper
- Cloves
- Cinnamon
- Licorice

Woody
- Smoky
- Oaky
- Vanilla

Earthy
- Old socks
- Musty
- Moldy

Weird
- Eggy
- Burnt match
- Cardboard

TASTES OF ....

....

....

Structure & Balance

THE ZIP (ACIDITY)
- ○ Low Buzz
- ○ Medium Bite
- ○ Lip-Tingling High

THE GRIP (TANNINS)
- ○ Big
- ○ Firm
- ○ Soft

THE OOMPH (BODY)
- ○ Light-bodied
- ○ Medium-bodied
- ○ Full-bodied

Three to five key words that will remind me what this wine was like ....

....

What I ate and how the wine matched ....

....

....

Takeaway tasting notes (look, smell, taste, and balance) ....

....

....

....

....

....

....

....

....

....

Date tasted ....

Okay   Pretty good   Will buy again

The Overview

WINE STYLE .... **COUNTRY** ....

GRAPE(S) .... **PRICE** ....

WINEMAKER (OR NAME OF PRODUCER) ....

Look, Smell & Taste

COLOR IS ....

SMELLS LIKE:

Fruity
- ○ Citrus
- ○ Tropical
- ○ Berry
- ○ Dried fruits

Veggie
- ○ Herby
- ○ Grassy
- ○ Green pepper
- ○ Minty

Bready
- ○ Yeasty

Floral
- ○ Orange blossom
- ○ Jasmine

Spicy
- ○ Pepper
- ○ Cloves
- ○ Cinnamon
- ○ Licorice

Woody
- ○ Smoky
- ○ Oaky
- ○ Vanilla

Earthy
- ○ Old socks
- ○ Musty
- ○ Moldy

Weird
- ○ Eggy
- ○ Burnt match
- ○ Cardboard

TASTES OF ....

....

....

Structure & Balance

THE ZIP (ACIDITY)
- Low Buzz
- Medium Bite
- Lip-Tingling High

THE GRIP (TANNINS)
- Big
- Firm
- Soft

THE OOMPH (BODY)
- Light-bodied
- Medium-bodied
- Full-bodied

Three to five key words that will remind me what this wine was like ....

....

What I ate and how the wine matched ....

....

....

Takeaway tasting notes (look, smell, taste, and balance) ....

....

....

....

....

....

....

....

....

Date tasted . . . .

Okay   Pretty good   Will buy again

The Overview

WINE STYLE . . . .   **COUNTRY** . . . .

GRAPE(S) . . . .   **PRICE** . . . .

WINEMAKER (OR NAME OF PRODUCER) . . . .

Look, Smell & Taste

COLOR IS . . . .

SMELLS LIKE:

Fruity
○ Citrus
○ Tropical
○ Berry
○ Dried fruits

Veggie
○ Herby
○ Grassy
○ Green pepper
○ Minty

Bready
○ Yeasty

Floral
○ Orange blossom
○ Jasmine

Spicy
○ Pepper
○ Cloves
○ Cinnamon
○ Licorice

Woody
○ Smoky
○ Oaky
○ Vanilla

Earthy
○ Old socks
○ Musty
○ Moldy

Weird
○ Eggy
○ Burnt match
○ Cardboard

TASTES OF . . . .

. . . .

. . . .

Structure & Balance

THE ZIP (ACIDITY)
- Low Buzz
- Medium Bite
- Lip-Tingling High

THE GRIP (TANNINS)
- Big
- Firm
- Soft

THE OOMPH (BODY)
- Light-bodied
- Medium-bodied
- Full-bodied

Three to five key words that will remind me what this wine was like ....

....

What I ate and how the wine matched ....

....

....

Takeaway tasting notes (look, smell, taste, and balance) ....

....

....

....

....

....

....

....

....

....

The Overview

WINE STYLE . . . .   **COUNTRY** . . . .

GRAPE(S) . . . .   **PRICE** . . . .

WINEMAKER (OR NAME OF PRODUCER) . . . .

Look, Smell & Taste

COLOR IS . . . .

SMELLS LIKE:

Fruity
○ Citrus
○ Tropical
○ Berry
○ Dried fruits

Veggie
○ Herby
○ Grassy
○ Green pepper
○ Minty

Bready
○ Yeasty

Floral
○ Orange blossom
○ Jasmine

Spicy
○ Pepper
○ Cloves
○ Cinnamon
○ Licorice

Woody
○ Smoky
○ Oaky
○ Vanilla

Earthy
○ Old socks
○ Musty
○ Moldy

Weird
○ Eggy
○ Burnt match
○ Cardboard

TASTES OF . . . .

. . . .

. . . .

Structure & Balance

THE ZIP (ACIDITY)
- Low Buzz
- Medium Bite
- Lip-Tingling High

THE GRIP (TANNINS)
- Big
- Firm
- Soft

THE OOMPH (BODY)
- Light-bodied
- Medium-bodied
- Full-bodied

Three to five key words that will remind me what this wine was like ....

....

What I ate and how the wine matched ....

....

....

Takeaway tasting notes (look, smell, taste, and balance) ....

....

....

....

....

....

....

....

....

Date tasted . . . .

Okay   Pretty good   Will buy again

The Overview

WINE STYLE . . . . **COUNTRY** . . . .

GRAPE(S) . . . . **PRICE** . . . .

WINEMAKER (OR NAME OF PRODUCER) . . . .

Look, Smell & Taste

COLOR IS . . . .

SMELLS LIKE:

Fruity
○ Citrus
○ Tropical
○ Berry
○ Dried fruits

Veggie
○ Herby
○ Grassy
○ Green pepper
○ Minty

Bready
○ Yeasty

Floral
○ Orange blossom
○ Jasmine

Spicy
○ Pepper
○ Cloves
○ Cinnamon
○ Licorice

Woody
○ Smoky
○ Oaky
○ Vanilla

Earthy
○ Old socks
○ Musty
○ Moldy

Weird
○ Eggy
○ Burnt match
○ Cardboard

TASTES OF . . . .

. . . .

. . . .

Structure & Balance

THE ZIP (ACIDITY)
- Low Buzz
- Medium Bite
- Lip-Tingling High

THE GRIP (TANNINS)
- Big
- Firm
- Soft

THE OOMPH (BODY)
- Light-bodied
- Medium-bodied
- Full-bodied

Three to five key words that will remind me what this wine was like

What I ate and how the wine matched

Takeaway tasting notes (look, smell, taste, and balance)

Date tasted . . . .

Okay   Pretty good   Will buy again

The Overview

WINE STYLE . . . . **COUNTRY** . . . .

GRAPE(S) . . . . **PRICE** . . . .

WINEMAKER (OR NAME OF PRODUCER) . . . .

Look, Smell & Taste

COLOR IS . . . .

SMELLS LIKE:

Fruity
- Citrus
- Tropical
- Berry
- Dried fruits

Veggie
- Herby
- Grassy
- Green pepper
- Minty

Bready
- Yeasty

Floral
- Orange blossom
- Jasmine

Spicy
- Pepper
- Cloves
- Cinnamon
- Licorice

Woody
- Smoky
- Oaky
- Vanilla

Earthy
- Old socks
- Musty
- Moldy

Weird
- Eggy
- Burnt match
- Cardboard

TASTES OF . . . .

. . . .

. . . .

Structure & Balance

THE ZIP (ACIDITY)
- Low Buzz
- Medium Bite
- Lip-Tingling High

THE GRIP (TANNINS)
- Big
- Firm
- Soft

THE OOMPH (BODY)
- Light-bodied
- Medium-bodied
- Full-bodied

Three to five key words that will remind me what this wine was like ....

....

What I ate and how the wine matched ....

....

....

Takeaway tasting notes (look, smell, taste, and balance) ....

....

....

....

....

....

....

....

....

Date tasted ....

☆ ☆ ☆ ☆ ☆

Okay   Pretty good   Will buy again

The Overview

WINE STYLE ....   **COUNTRY** ....

GRAPE(S) ....   **PRICE** ....

WINEMAKER (OR NAME OF PRODUCER) ....

Look, Smell & Taste

COLOR IS ....

SMELLS LIKE:

Fruity
○ Citrus
○ Tropical
○ Berry
○ Dried fruits

Veggie
○ Herby
○ Grassy
○ Green pepper
○ Minty

Bready
○ Yeasty

Floral
○ Orange blossom
○ Jasmine

Spicy
○ Pepper
○ Cloves
○ Cinnamon
○ Licorice

Woody
○ Smoky
○ Oaky
○ Vanilla

Earthy
○ Old socks
○ Musty
○ Moldy

Weird
○ Eggy
○ Burnt match
○ Cardboard

TASTES OF ....

....

....

Structure & Balance

THE ZIP (ACIDITY)
○ Low Buzz
○ Medium Bite
○ Lip-Tingling High

THE GRIP (TANNINS)
○ Big
○ Firm
○ Soft

THE OOMPH (BODY)
○ Light-bodied
○ Medium-bodied
○ Full-bodied

Three to five key words that will remind me what this wine was like ....

....

What I ate and how the wine matched ....

....

....

Takeaway tasting notes (look, smell, taste, and balance) ....

....

....

....

....

....

....

....

....

Date tasted ....

Okay   Pretty good   Will buy again

The Overview

WINE STYLE ....   **COUNTRY** ....

GRAPE(S) ....   **PRICE** ....

WINEMAKER (OR NAME OF PRODUCER) ....

Look, Smell & Taste

COLOR IS ....

SMELLS LIKE:

Fruity
- ○ Citrus
- ○ Tropical
- ○ Berry
- ○ Dried fruits

Veggie
- ○ Herby
- ○ Grassy
- ○ Green pepper
- ○ Minty

Bready
- ○ Yeasty

Floral
- ○ Orange blossom
- ○ Jasmine

Spicy
- ○ Pepper
- ○ Cloves
- ○ Cinnamon
- ○ Licorice

Woody
- ○ Smoky
- ○ Oaky
- ○ Vanilla

Earthy
- ○ Old socks
- ○ Musty
- ○ Moldy

Weird
- ○ Eggy
- ○ Burnt match
- ○ Cardboard

TASTES OF ....

....

....

Structure & Balance

THE ZIP (ACIDITY)
- ○ Low Buzz
- ○ Medium Bite
- ○ Lip-Tingling High

THE GRIP (TANNINS)
- ○ Big
- ○ Firm
- ○ Soft

THE OOMPH (BODY)
- ○ Light-bodied
- ○ Medium-bodied
- ○ Full-bodied

Three to five key words that will remind me what this wine was like ....

....

What I ate and how the wine matched ....

....

....

Takeaway tasting notes (look, smell, taste, and balance) ....

....

....

....

....

....

....

....

....

Date tasted ....

Okay   Pretty good   Will buy again

The Overview

WINE STYLE .... **COUNTRY** ....

GRAPE(S) .... **PRICE** ....

WINEMAKER (OR NAME OF PRODUCER) ....

Look, Smell & Taste

COLOR IS ....

SMELLS LIKE:

Fruity
○ Citrus
○ Tropical
○ Berry
○ Dried fruits

Veggie
○ Herby
○ Grassy
○ Green pepper
○ Minty

Bready
○ Yeasty

Floral
○ Orange blossom
○ Jasmine

Spicy
○ Pepper
○ Cloves
○ Cinnamon
○ Licorice

Woody
○ Smoky
○ Oaky
○ Vanilla

Earthy
○ Old socks
○ Musty
○ Moldy

Weird
○ Eggy
○ Burnt match
○ Cardboard

TASTES OF ....

....

....